YOUR JOURNEY with GOD Through CANCER

and Beyond

Scripture quotations are taken from:

The Holy Bible, King James Version (KJV)

The Holy Bible, New International Version (NIV) Copyright © 1973, 1978, 1984, by International Bible Society. Used by permission of Zondervan Publishing House. All rights reserved.

The Holy Bible, New King James Version (NKJV) Copyright © 1982 by Thomas Nelson, Inc. Used by permission.

Holy Bible, New Living Translation, (NLT) copyright © 1996. Used by permission of Tyndale House Publishers, Inc., Wheaton, Illinois 60189. All rights reserved.

The Message (MSG)- This edition issued by contractual arrangement with NavPress, a division of The Navigators, U.S.A. Originally published by NavPress in English as THE MESSAGE: The Bible in Contemporary Language copyright 2002-2003 by Eugene Peterson. All rights reserved.

New Century Version®. (NCV) Copyright © 1987, 1988, 1991 by Word Publishing, a division of Thomas Nelson, Inc. All rights reserved. Used by permission.

The New American Standard Bible®, (NASB) Copyright © 1960, 1962, 1963, 1968, 1971, 1972, 1973, 1975, 1977, 1995 by The Lockman Foundation. Used by permission.

International Children's Bible®, New Century Version®. (ICB) Copyright © 1986, 1988, 1999 by Tommy Nelson™, a division of Thomas Nelson, Inc. All rights reserved. Used by permission.

The Holman Christian Standard Bible™ (HOLMAN CSB) Copyright © 1999, 2000, 2001 by Holman Bible Publishers. Used by permission.

Cover Design by Kim Russell / Wahoo Designs
Page Layout by Bart Dawson

ISBN 978-1-60587-164-6

Printed in the United States of America

YOUR JOURNEY with GOD Through CANCER

365 DAILY DEVOTIONS AND JOURNAL

and Beyond

These things I have spoken to you,
that in Me you may have peace.
In the world you will have tribulation;
but be of good cheer,
I have overcome the world.

—

John 16:33 NKJV

INTRODUCTION

Physically, cancer is an endurance contest—spiritually it is a journey. As you make that journey through and beyond your illness, you'll undoubtedly learn lessons about yourself, about your faith, and about your Creator. This book is intended to help.

This text contains 365 chapters, one for each day of the year. During the next 12 months, try this experiment: read a chapter each day—and while you're at it, try jotting down your own ideas on the space provided at the conclusion of each chapter.

When you talk to God every day, He will fill your heart, He will direct your thoughts, and He will guide your steps.

Do you have questions that you can't answer? God has answers. Do you have fears about the future? God offers hope. Do you want to be a better person, a better patient, and a better Christian? If so, ask for God's help and ask for it many times each day . . . starting with a regular, heartfelt morning devotional. Even a few minutes each morning is enough time to change your day . . . and your life.

THROUGH AND BEYOND CANCER

Trust in the Lord with all your heart, and do not rely on your own understanding; think about Him in all your ways, and He will guide you on the right paths.

Proverbs 3:5-6 Holman CSB

The journey through and beyond your illness is a physical struggle, no doubt. But it's also a spiritual struggle and a test of faith. And, it's a journey you should make with God.

God has given you this day, and He has filled it to the brim with both challenges and possibilities. If you're facing a difficult day or a tough round of treatments, have faith, have courage, and trust your Heavenly Father. When you do, you can be comforted in the knowledge that your Creator is both loving and wise, and that He understands His plans perfectly, even when you do not.

———

God is God. Because He is God, He is worthy of my trust and obedience. I will find rest nowhere but in His holy will, a will that is unspeakably beyond my largest notions of what He is up to.

Elisabeth Elliot

—Your Thoughts for Today—

a ... yet ...
... The dis-
ease is overwhelming.

SPENDING TIME WITH GOD EVERY DAY

Do not have other gods besides Me.

Exodus 20:3 Holman CSB

As you make the difficult journey through and beyond your illness, you'll be wise to spend quality time with God every day. When you do, it will change your life and might just change the course of your recovery.

When you begin each day with your head bowed and your heart lifted, you remind yourself of God's love, His protection, and His commandments. And if you are wise, you will use your morning prayer time to align your priorities for the coming day with the teachings and commandments of God's Holy Word. So as you make the journey through and beyond your illness, carve out time for the Father every morning. He deserves it . . . and so do you.

Are you weak? Weary? Confused? Troubled? Pressured? How is your relationship with God? Is it held in its place of priority? I believe the greater the pressure, the greater your need for time alone with Him.

Kay Arthur

—Your Thoughts for Today—

STRENGTH FOR THE JOURNEY

Finally, be strengthened by the Lord and by His vast strength.
Ephesians 6:10 Holman CSB

There's no doubt about it: cancer is exhausting, both physically and mentally. So when you feel too tired to take another step, where will you turn for strength? You should turn to God.

Your Heavenly Father offers strength for any trial and peace that passes understanding. Claim His strength today. And accept His peace. When you do, you'll soon discover that you can do things with God that you could never do without Him.

Notice what Jesus had to say concerning those who have wearied themselves by trying to do things in their own strength: "Come to me, all you who labor and are heavy laden, and I will give you rest."

Henry Blackaby and Claude King

—Your Thoughts for Today—

HE OFFERS HOPE

Now may the God of hope fill you with all joy and peace in believing, that you may abound in hope by the power of the Holy Spirit.

Romans 15:13 NKJV

The hope that the world offers is fleeting and imperfect. The hope that God offers is unchanging, unshakable, and unending. It is no wonder, then, that when we seek security from worldly sources, our hopes are often dashed. Thankfully, God has no such record of failure.

Where will you place your hopes today? Will you entrust your future to man or to God? Will you seek solace exclusively from fallible human beings, or will you place your hopes, first and foremost, in the trusting hands of your Creator? The decision is yours, and you must live with the results of the choice you make.

For thoughtful believers, hope begins with God. Period. So today, as you embark upon the next stage of your journey through and beyond your illness, consider the words of the Psalmist: "You are my hope; O Lord GOD, You are my confidence" (71:5 NASB). Then, place your trust in the One who cannot be shaken.

—Your Thoughts for Today—

Things have to get better. I'm
trying to keep faith that God wants
me to recover from this ordeal
somehow.

OPTIMISM MATTERS

My cup runs over. Surely goodness and mercy shall follow me all the days of my life; and I will dwell in the house of the Lord Forever.

Psalm 23:5-6 NKJV

If you believe in an all-knowing, all-loving God, then you'll find it hard to be a pessimist. After all, with God in His heaven, and with God on your side, you have every reason to live courageously. Yet you're only human, so from time to time you may, fall prey to fear, doubt, or discouragement. If so, it's time to lift your hopes and your prayers to God.

Time and again the Bible reminds us of God's blessings. In response to His grace, we should strive to focus our thoughts on things that are pleasing to Him, not upon things that are corrupting, discouraging, or frustrating.

So, the next time you find yourself mired in the pit of pessimism, remember God's Word and redirect your thoughts. This world is God's creation; look for the best in it—when you do, you won't need to look very far to find it.

The Christian lifestyle is not one of legalistic do's and don'ts, but one that is positive, attractive, and joyful.

Vonette Bright

—Your Thoughts for Today—

This treatment today felt much better, and I'm working to get my energy back.

YOUR PARTNERSHIP WITH GOD

The Lord is with you when you are with Him. If you seek Him, He will be found by you.

2 Chronicles 15:2 Holman CSB

As you make the journey through and beyond cancer—a difficult journey to be sure—you need a partner. That Partner is God. And the good news is this: When you humbly and sincerely ask God to become your partner, He will grant your request and transform your life.

Is your life a testimony to the personal relationship that you enjoy with your Heavenly Father? Or have you compartmentalized your faith to a few hours on Sunday morning? If you genuinely wish to make God your full-time partner, you must allow Him to reign over every aspect of your life and every day of your week. When you do, you'll be amazed at the things that the two of you, working together, can accomplish.

———

There's not much you can't achieve or endure if you know God is walking by your side. Just remember: Someone knows, and Someone cares.

Bill Hybels

—Your Thoughts for Today—

IN HIS HANDS

For whatever is born of God overcomes the world. And this is the victory that has overcome the world—our faith.

1 John 5:4 NKJV

The first element of a successful life is faith: faith in God, faith in His Son, and faith in His promises. If we place our lives in God's hands, our faith is rewarded in ways that we—as human beings with clouded vision and limited understanding—can scarcely comprehend. But, if we seek to rely solely upon our own resources, or if we seek earthly success outside the boundaries of God's commandments, we reap an unfortunate harvest for ourselves and for our loved ones.

Do you desire the abundance and success that God has promised? Then trust Him today and every day that you live. Then, when you have entrusted your future to the Giver of all things good, rest assured that your future is secure, not only for today, but also for all eternity.

Faith is the gaze of a soul upon a saving God.

A. W. Tozer

—Your Thoughts for Today—

CALMING YOUR FEARS

Be not afraid; only believe.

Mark 5:36 NKJV

Cancer. It's a word that can strike fear in the most courageous heart. So it's no surprise that cancer and fear are often traveling companions.

Are you fearful about your future? Are you concerned about the inevitable challenges of your journey back to health? If so, it's time to take your fears to God . . . and leave them there.

Today, ask God to help you regain a clear perspective about the problems (and opportunities) that confront you. When you petition your Heavenly Father sincerely and seek His guidance, He can touch your heart, clear your vision, renew your mind, and calm your fears.

The fierce grip of panic need not immobilize you. God knows no limitation when it comes to deliverance. Admit your fear. Commit it to Him. Dump the pressure on Him. He can handle it.

Charles Swindoll

—Your Thoughts for Today—

BEYOND THE STRESS

We wait for the Lord; He is our help and shield.

Psalm 33:20 Holman CSB

Face facts: cancer is stressful . . . very stressful. As you move through and beyond your illness, the question is not whether you'll encounter stress, but how you'll choose to deal with it. You can either tackle things on your own, or you can enlist God's help.

Today, make God a full partner in your life and your treatment. When you do, He will calm your fears and guide your steps. So instead of focusing on the world, focus, instead, on God and upon His will for your life. Seek His wisdom and His help. And remember: No challenge is too great for Him. Not even yours.

The damage done to us on this earth will never find its way into that safe city. We can relax, we can rest, and though some of us can hardly imagine it, we can prepare to feel safe and secure for all of eternity.

Bill Hybels

—Your Thoughts for Today—

MEETING THE CHALLENGES OF LIFE

Therefore, get your minds ready for action, being self-disciplined, and set your hope completely on the grace to be brought to you at the revelation of Jesus Christ.

1 Peter 1:13 Holman CSB

Cancer is a life-changing experience. It provokes fear; it causes anxiety; it may shake your faith and cloud your vision of the future. But as a Christian, you need not be afraid. After all, God loves you, and He has promised to protect you today, tomorrow, and forever.

So as you walk through the darker valleys of life, always keep your eyes focused on the mountaintops up ahead. Remember that God will never abandon you. In times of hardship, He will comfort you; in times of change, He will guide your steps. When you are troubled, or weak, or sorrowful, God's love will encircle you. In a world that is constantly changing, you must build your life on the rock that cannot be moved...you must trust in God. Always.

———

God will lead you through, not around, the valley.

Max Lucado

—Your Thoughts for Today—

_____

_____

_____

_____

FEELING NUMB

Be still, and know that I am God.

Psalm 46:10 NKJV

I f you're just beginning your journey through and beyond cancer, you may be surprised, not by the intensity of your emotions, but by the lack of them. If so, you should know that emotional numbness is a common response to any significant loss, especially in the early stages of the grieving process.

So, if you're feeling numb, don't think you're the only person who's ever felt that way. And if you're still in a state of disbelief, don't shut yourself off from your loved ones. Keep talking to your family, to your friends, and to God. When you do, you'll discover that talking about your grief, while painful at first, can be helpful in the long run.

When the full impact of our loss hit home, it seemed that everything moved in slow motion.

Zig Ziglar

—Your Thoughts for Today—

_____

_____

_____

_____

_____

_____

EMOTIONAL QUICKSAND

He will wipe away every tear from their eyes. Death will exist no longer; grief, crying, and pain will exist no longer, because the previous things have passed away.

Revelation 21:4 Holman CSB

When you find yourself caught in the emotional quicksand called grief, you may wonder if you'll ever recover. When the feelings of sorrow are intense, you may think—mistakenly—that the pain will never subside. But the good news is this: while time heals many wounds, God has the power to heal them all.

God's Holy Word makes it clear: absolutely nothing is impossible for Him. And since the Bible means what it says, you can be comforted in the knowledge that the Creator of the universe can do miraculous things in your own life and in the lives of your loved ones. Your challenge, as a believer, is to take God at His word, and to wait patiently for Him to bless you with peace that flows from His miraculous healing touch.

In times of deepest suffering it is the faithful carrying out of ordinary duties that brings the greatest consolation.

Elisabeth Elliot

—Your Thoughts for Today—

WHERE TO FIND COURAGE

Cast your burden on the Lord, and He will support you; He will never allow the righteous to be shaken.

Psalm 55:22 Holman CSB

Christians have every reason to live courageously. After all, the ultimate battle has already been won on the cross at Calvary. But even dedicated followers of Christ may find their courage tested by the inevitable disappointments and fears that visit the lives of believers and non-believers alike.

As you make the journey through and beyond the diagnosis of cancer, you may find yourself worried about the challenges of today or the uncertainties of tomorrow. During times of uncertainty, you must ask yourself whether or not you are ready to place your concerns and your life in God's all-powerful, all-knowing, all-loving hands. If the answer to that question is yes—as it should be—then you can draw courage today from the source of strength that never fails: your Heavenly Father.

———

The Lord is glad to open the gate to every knocking soul. It opens freely; no bolts secure it. Have faith and enter at this moment through holy courage. If you knock with a heavy heart, you shall yet sing with joy of spirit. Never be discouraged!

C. H. Spurgeon

—Your Thoughts for Today—

_____

_____

_____

CONQUERING EVERYDAY FRUSTRATIONS

A hot-tempered man stirs up conflict, but a man slow to anger calms strife.

Proverbs 15:18 Holman CSB

Sorting through the red tape of our modern medical bureaucracy can be frustrating, but it need not be devastating. After all, when compared to the vastness of eternity, today's problems aren't ever as big as they seem.

As long as you live here on earth, you will face countless opportunities to lose your temper over small, relatively insignificant events such as an inconsiderate comment, or an inarticulate doctor, or an incorrect hospital bill. When you are tempted to lose your temper over these things, don't. Turn away from anger and turn, instead, to God. When you do, you'll be following His commandments and giving yourself a priceless gift . . . the gift of peace.

When you strike out in anger, you may miss the other person, but you will always hit yourself.

Jim Gallery

—Your Thoughts for Today—

INFINITE POSSIBILITIES

Is anything too hard for the LORD?

Genesis 18:14 KJV

Ours is a God of infinite possibilities. But sometimes, because of limited faith and limited understanding, we wrongly assume that God cannot or will not intervene in the affairs of mankind. Such assumptions are simply wrong.

Are you afraid to ask God for physical, spiritual, or emotional healing? If so, it's time to abandon your doubts and reclaim your faith in God's promises.

God's Holy Word makes it clear: absolutely nothing is impossible for the Lord. And since the Bible means what it says, you can be comforted in the knowledge that the Creator of the universe can do miraculous things in your own life and in the lives of your loved ones. Your challenge, as a believer, is to take God at His word, and to expect the miraculous.

God has power and He's willing to share it if we step out in faith and believe that He will.

Bill Hybels

—Your Thoughts for Today—

ETERNAL PERSPECTIVE

Our Savior Jesus poured out new life so generously. God's gift has restored our relationship with him and given us back our lives. And there's more life to come—an eternity of life!

Titus 3:6-7 MSG

As you make the journey through cancer treatment and beyond, it's easy to lose perspective. After all, you may be faced with unfamiliar treatments, unrelenting pressures, and an uncertain future. But when times are tough, it's always good to slow down, step back, and look at things from God's perspective.

Your Heavenly Father sees your life from an eternal perspective. And, He knows that you're protected, now and forever. So the next time you feel overwhelmed by the demands of life, or treatment, or both, compare the length and severity of today's troubles with the vast scope of eternal life. When you do, you'll keep today's problems in proper perspective.

All that is not eternal is eternally out of date.

C. S. Lewis

—Your Thoughts for Today—

DISCOVERING GOD'S PLANS

For it is God who is working among you both the willing and the working for His good purpose.

Philippians 2:13 Holman CSB

Throughout your journey through illness and beyond, God has a plan for you, a way that He can use your experiences for His glory. If you seek to discover God's plan for your life—and you should—then you will live in accordance with His commandments. You will study God's Word, and you will be watchful for His signs. You will associate with fellow Christians who will encourage your spiritual growth, and you will listen to that inner voice that speaks to you in the quiet moments of your daily devotionals.

God intends to use you in surprising ways if you let Him. The decision to seek God's plan and to follow it is yours and yours alone. The consequences of that decision have implications that are both profound and eternal, so choose carefully.

God has a plan for the life of every Christian. Every circumstance, every turn of destiny, all things work together for your good and for His glory.

Billy Graham

—Your Thoughts for Today—

_____

_____

_____

_____

BE ASSERTIVE

For God has not given us a spirit of fearfulness, but one of power, love, and sound judgment.

2 Timothy 1:7 Holman CSB

A s you make the journey through and beyond cancer, you'll sometimes need to be assertive. The medical maze can be puzzling, and when you have questions, you should never hesitate to ask the doctors for the answers you need.

When Paul wrote Timothy, he reminded his young protégé that the God they served was a bold God, and God's spirit empowered His children with boldness also. Like Timothy, we all must face times of uncertainty and fear. God's message is the same to us, today, as it was to Timothy: We can live boldly because the spirit of God resides in us.

So today, as you face the challenges of living with— and overcoming—cancer, remember that God is with you . . . and you are protected. So be bold, be brave, and be assertive.

———

Jesus is not a strong man making men and women who gather around Him weak. He is the Strong creating the strong.

E. Stanley Jones

—Your Thoughts for Today—

_____

_____

_____

THE SHEPHERD'S CARE

Your righteousness reaches heaven, God, You who have done great things; God, who is like You?

Psalm 71:19 Holman CSB

I t's a promise that is made over and over again in the Bible: Whatever "it" is, God can handle it.

Life isn't always easy. Far from it! Sometimes, life can be very, very difficult. But even then, even during our darkest moments, we're protected by a loving Heavenly Father. When we're worried, God can reassure us; when we're sad, God can comfort us. When our hearts are broken, God is not just near, He is here. So we must lift our thoughts and prayers to Him. When we do, He will answer our prayers. Why? Because He is our Shepherd, and He has promised to protect us now and forever.

He is always thinking about us. We are before his eyes. The Lord's eye never sleeps, but is always watching out for our welfare. We are continually on his heart.

C. H. Spurgeon

—Your Thoughts for Today—

_____

_____

_____

_____

_____

_____

IN TIMES OF ADVERSITY

For whatever is born of God overcomes the world. And this is the victory that has overcome the world—our faith.

1 John 5:4 NKJV

Few experiences in life are more difficult than dealing with a diagnosis of cancer. The journey through and beyond serious illness can be daunting. Thankfully, the reassuring words of 1 John 5:4 remind us that when we accept God's grace, we overcome the passing hardships of this world by relying upon His strength, His love, and His promise of eternal life.

When we face the inevitable difficulties of life-here-on-earth, God stands ready to protect us. Our responsibility, of course, is to ask Him for protection. When we call upon Him in heartfelt prayer, He will answer—in His own time and according to His own plan—and He will heal us. And while we are waiting for God's plans to unfold and for His healing touch to restore us, we can be comforted in the knowledge that our Creator can overcome any obstacle, even if we cannot. Let us take God at His word, and let us trust Him.

—Your Thoughts for Today—

BEYOND BITTERNESS

All bitterness, anger and wrath, insult and slander must be removed from you, along with all wickedness. And be kind and compassionate to one another, forgiving one another, just as God also forgave you in Christ.

Ephesians 4:31-32 Holman CSB

H as your illness left you mired in the quicksand of bitterness or regret? If so, you are not alone. Bitterness can be a natural outgrowth of any serious illness, but it need not be.

If you are angry with God, reject those feelings. Or, if you are embittered against yourself for past mistakes or shortcomings, forgive yourself and move on. Bitterness and regret are not part of God's plan for your life. So move beyond bitterness. Today.

Bitterness is the greatest barrier to friendship with God.

Rick Warren

—Your Thoughts for Today—

EXPRESSING YOUR EMOTIONS

Blessed are those who mourn, for they shall be comforted.

Matthew 5:4 NKJV

In the Old Testament, Job's example teaches us that it's okay to express grief. Job cried bitter tears; he cursed the day he was born (Job 3:1-3); he expressed questions that he could not answer; and he gave voice to his suffering. But he never grieved alone. When everyone else failed him, including friends and family, Job knew that God still ruled over the entire world and over Job's own corner of the world. Job trusted that God was always present . . . and so should you.

God gave you emotions, and He intends for you to use them. When you express your emotions sincerely, you will begin the process of healing. But if you suppress your emotions or if you ignore your feelings altogether, you may needlessly prolong your pain.

So, if you have experienced a significant loss or a profound disappointment, don't bottle up everything inside. Express your feelings; talk openly to loved ones; allow tears to flow. Even if you'd rather ignore your pain, don't do it. Instead, reach out to the people you love and trust.

By honestly expressing yourself, you will take an active role in God's plan for your recovery. And in time, you'll experience the comfort and the joy that can—and should—be yours.

There is no way around suffering. We have to go through it to get to the other side.

Barbara Johnson

If we are not willing to feel negative emotions, then we shall not experience the richness of our positive emotions.

C. S. Lewis

Christians are told not to stifle their grief or to behave unscripturally stoic.

Charles Stanley

When we cry, we allow our bodies to function according to God's design—and we embrace one of the "perks" he offers to relieve our stress.

Barbara Johnson

—Your Thoughts for Today—

_____

_____

_____

_____

_____

_____

_____

_____

_____

_____

_____

WHERE TO TAKE YOUR WORRIES

Don't worry about anything, but in everything, through prayer and petition with thanksgiving, let your requests be made known to God.

Philippians 4:6 Holman CSB

Where is the best place to take your worries? Take them to God. Take your troubles to Him; take your fears to Him; take your doubts to Him; take your weaknesses to Him; take your sorrows to Him . . . and leave them all there. Seek protection from the One who offers you eternal salvation; build your spiritual house upon the Rock that cannot be moved.

Today, remember that God still sits in His heaven and you are His beloved child. Then, perhaps, you will worry a little less and trust God a little more, and that's as it should be because God is trustworthy…and you are protected.

———

Worry makes you forget who's in charge.

Max Lucado

—Your Thoughts for Today—

_____

_____

_____

_____

_____

SPIRITUAL GROWTH

Therefore, leaving the elementary message about the Messiah, let us go on to maturity.

Hebrews 6:1 Holman CSB

The journey through and beyond cancer is both a physical and a spiritual journey. And it's worth noting that the journey toward spiritual maturity lasts a lifetime. As Christians, we can and should continue to grow in the love and the knowledge of our Savior as long as we live. Norman Vincent Peale had the following advice for believers of all ages: "Ask the God who made you to keep remaking you." That advice, of course, is perfectly sound, but often ignored.

When we cease to grow, either emotionally or spiritually, we do ourselves a profound disservice. But, if we study God's Word, if we obey His commandments, and if we live in the center of His will, we will not be "stagnant" believers; we will, instead, be growing Christians . . . and that's exactly what God wants for our lives.

The almighty Father will use life's reverses to move you forward.

Barbara Johnson

—Your Thoughts for Today—

_____

_____

_____

_____

ASK AND RECEIVE

Ask, and it will be given to you; seek, and you will find; knock, and it will be opened to you. For everyone who asks receives, and he who seeks finds, and to him who knocks it will be opened.

Matthew 7:7-8 NKJV

Are you a person who asks God for guidance and strength? If so, then you're continually inviting your Creator to reveal Himself in a variety of ways. As a follower of Christ, you must do no less.

Today, reach out to the Giver of all blessings. Turn to Him for guidance and for strength. Invite Him into every corner of your day. Ask Him to teach you and to lead you. And remember that no matter your circumstances, God is never far away; He is with you always.

So, whatever your need, no matter how great or small, pray about it and never lose hope. God is not just near; He is here, and He's perfectly capable of answering your prayers. Now, it's up to you to ask.

We honor God by asking for great things when they are a part of His promise. We dishonor Him and cheat ourselves when we ask for molehills where He has promised mountains.

Vance Havner

—Your Thoughts for Today—

FINDING PEACE

For the mind-set of the flesh is death, but the mind-set of the Spirit is life and peace.

Romans 8:6 Holman CSB

Sometimes, peace can be a scarce commodity as we endure life's inevitable hardships. How, then, can we find the peace that we so desperately desire? By turning our days and our lives over to God.

The Scottish preacher George McDonald observed, "It has been well said that no man ever sank under the burden of the day. It is when tomorrow's burden is added to the burden of today that the weight is more than a man can bear. Never load yourselves so, my friends. If you find yourselves so loaded, at least remember this: it is your own doing, not God's. He begs you to leave the future to Him."

May we give our lives, our hopes, our prayers, and our futures to the Father, and, by doing so, accept His will and His peace.

We're prone to want God to change our circumstances, but He wants to change our character. We think that peace comes from the outside in, but it comes from the inside out.

Warren Wiersbe

—Your Thoughts for Today—

_____

_____

_____

A PASSION FOR LIFE

But those who trust in the Lord will renew their strength;
they will soar on wings like eagles; they will run and not grow
weary; they will walk and not faint.

Isaiah 40:31 Holman CSB

A re you enthusiastic about your life, your faith, and your journey back to health? Hopefully so. But if your zest for life has waned, it is now time to redirect your efforts and recharge your spiritual batteries. And that means refocusing your priorities (by putting God first) and counting your blessings (instead of your troubles).

Nothing is more important than your wholehearted commitment to your Creator and to His only begotten Son. Your faith must never be an afterthought; it must be your ultimate priority, your ultimate possession, and your ultimate passion. When you become passionate about your faith, you'll become passionate about your life, too. And God will smile.

I don't know about you, but I want to do more than survive life—I want to mount up like the eagle and soar on the wings of the wind.

Barbara Johnson

—Your Thoughts for Today—

NO IMPOSSIBILITIES

For nothing will be impossible with God.

Luke 1:37 Holman CSB

God promises that all things are possible through Him, and He promises that He can work miracles in the lives of those who trust Him. Count yourself among that number today and every day of your life.

When you put absolute faith in God, you avail yourself of His power and His peace. And when you take God at His word—when you believe that absolutely nothing is impossible for Him—you'll be amazed at the things He can do.

So today, as you fulfill the responsibilities of everyday life, expect God to do big things for you and yours. Trust that the Creator of the universe is capable of moving any mountain, including your own. And don't ever be afraid to ask for a miracle in His name.

We have a God who delights in impossibilities.

Andrew Murray

—Your Thoughts for Today—

_____

_____

_____

_____

_____

_____

CONSIDERING THE CROSS

But God forbid that I should boast except in the cross of our Lord Jesus Christ, by whom the world has been crucified to me, and I to the world.

Galatians 6:14 NKJV

As we consider Christ's sacrifice on the cross, we should be profoundly humbled and profoundly grateful. And today, as we come to Christ in prayer, we should do so in a spirit of quiet, heartfelt devotion to the One who gave His life so that we might have life eternal.

He was the Son of God, but He wore a crown of thorns. He was the Savior of mankind, yet He was put to death on roughhewn cross made of wood. He offered His healing touch to an unsaved world, and yet the same hands that had healed the sick and raised the dead were pierced with nails.

Christ humbled Himself on a cross—for you. As you approach Him today in prayer, think about His love and His sacrifice. And be grateful.

The heaviest end of the cross lies ever on His shoulders. If He bids us carry a burden, He carries it also.

C. H. Spurgeon

—Your Thoughts for Today—

SAFETY FROM THE STORM

But He said to them, "Why are you fearful, you of little faith?" Then He got up and rebuked the winds and the sea. And there was a great calm.

Matthew 8:26 Holman CSB

Sometimes, we feel threatened by the storms of life. During these moments, when our hearts are flooded with uncertainty, we must remember that God is not simply near, He is here.

Have you ever felt your faith in God slipping away? If so, you are in good company. Even the most faithful Christians are, at times, beset by occasional bouts of discouragement and doubt. But even when you feel far removed from God, God never leaves your side. He is always with you. When you sincerely seek His presence— and when you genuinely seek to establish a deeper, more meaningful relationship with His Son—God will calm your fears, answer your prayers, and restore your soul.

It is the trial of our faith that is precious. If we go through the trial, there is so much wealth laid up in our heavenly bank account to draw upon when the next test comes.

Oswald Chambers

—Your Thoughts for Today—

LIFE ETERNAL

In a little while the world will see Me no longer, but you will see Me. Because I live, you will live too.

John 14:19 Holman CSB

How marvelous it is that God became a man and walked among us. Had He not chosen to do so, we might feel removed from a distant Creator. But ours is not a distant God. Ours is a God who understands—far better than we ever could—the essence of what it means to be human.

God understands our hopes, our fears, and our temptations. He understands what it means to be angry and what it costs to forgive. He knows the heart, the conscience, and the soul of every person who has ever lived, including you. And God has a plan of salvation that is intended for you. Accept it. Accept God's gift through the person of His Son Christ Jesus, and then rest assured: God walked among us so that you might have eternal life; amazing though it may seem, He did it for you.

———

Let us see the victorious Jesus: the conqueror of the tomb, the one who defied death. And let us be reminded that we, too, will be granted the same victory!

Max Lucado

If you are a believer, your judgment will not determine your eternal destiny. Christ's finished work on Calvary was applied to you the moment you accepted Christ as Savior.

Beth Moore

God has promised us abundance, peace, and eternal life. These treasures are ours for the asking; all we must do is claim them. One of the great mysteries of life is why on earth do so many of us wait so very long to lay claim to God's gifts?

Marie T. Freeman

And because we know Christ is alive, we have hope for the present and hope for life beyond the grave.

Billy Graham

God's riches are beyond anything we could ask or even dare to imagine!

Barbara Johnson

—Your Thoughts for Today—

RELYING UPON HIM

Humble yourselves therefore under the mighty hand of God, so that He may exalt you in due time, casting all your care upon Him, because He cares about you.

1 Peter 5:6-7 Holman CSB

God is a never-ending source of support and courage for those of us who call upon Him. When we are weary, He gives us strength. When we see no hope, God reminds us of His promises. When we grieve, God wipes away our tears.

Do the demands of your treatment threaten to overwhelm you? If so, you must rely not only upon your own resources but also upon the promises of your Father in heaven. God will hold your hand and walk with you every day of your life if you let Him. So even if your circumstances are difficult, trust the Father. His love is eternal and His goodness endures forever.

———

Faith is not merely you holding on to God—it is God holding on to you.

E. Stanley Jones

—Your Thoughts for Today—

_____

_____

_____

_____

_____

_____

GOD'S TIMETABLE

Therefore humble yourselves under the mighty hand of God, that He may exalt you in due time.

1 Peter 5:6 NKJV

Sometimes, the hardest thing to do is to wait, especially when we're waiting to get well. We would prefer instantaneous healing, but the journey through cancer and beyond takes time. So we must be patient, and we must be strong.

Billy Graham observed, "As we wait on God, He helps us use the winds of adversity to soar above our problems." So today, as you meet the challenges of life and the challenges of your illness, do your best to turn everything over to God. Whatever "it" is, He can handle it. And you can be sure that He will handle it when the time is right.

God has a designated time when his promise will be fulfilled and the prayer will be answered.

Jim Cymbala

—Your Thoughts for Today—

THE WORLD'S BEST FRIEND

No one has greater love than this, that someone would lay down his life for his friends.

John 15:13 Holman CSB

Who's the best friend this world has ever had? Jesus, of course. And when you form a life-changing relationship with Him, He will be your best friend, too . . . your friend forever.

Jesus has offered to share the gifts of everlasting life and everlasting love with the world and with you. If you make mistakes, He'll stand by you. If you fall short of His commandments, He'll still love you. If you feel lonely or worried, He can touch your heart and lift your spirits.

Jesus wants you to enjoy a happy, healthy, abundant life. He wants you to walk with Him and to share His Good News. You can do it. And with a friend like Jesus, you will.

The dearest friend on earth is but a mere shadow compared with Jesus Christ.

Oswald Chambers

—Your Thoughts for Today—

UP FOR THE CHALLENGE

I will be your God throughout your lifetime—until your hair is white with age. I made you, and I will care for you. I will carry you along and save you.

Isaiah 46:4 NLT

God has promised to lift you up and guide your steps if you let Him do so. God has promised that when you entrust your life to Him completely and without reservation, He will give you the strength to meet any challenge, the courage to face any trial, and the wisdom to live in His righteousness.

God's hand uplifts those who turn their hearts and prayers to Him. Will you count yourself among that number? Will you accept God's peace and wear God's armor against the temptations and distractions of our dangerous world? If you do, you can live courageously and optimistically, knowing that you have been forever touched by the loving, unfailing, uplifting hand of God.

The God of the galaxies is the God who knows when your heart is broken—and He can heal it!

Warren Wiersbe

—Your Thoughts for Today—

TRUST THE SHEPHERD

The LORD is my shepherd; I shall not want. He maketh me to lie down in green pastures: he leadeth me beside the still waters. He restoreth my soul: he leadeth me in the paths of righteousness for his name's sake. Yea, though I walk through the valley of the shadow of death, I will fear no evil: for thou art with me; thy rod and thy staff they comfort me. Thou preparest a table before me in the presence of mine enemies: thou anointest my head with oil; my cup runneth over. Surely goodness and mercy shall follow me all the days of my life: and I will dwell in the house of the LORD for ever.

Psalm 23 KJV

On occasion, you will confront circumstances that trouble you to the very core of your soul. When you are afraid, trust in God. When you are worried, turn your concerns over to Him. When you are anxious, be still and listen for the quiet assurance of God's promises. And then, place your life in His hands. He is your Shepherd today and throughout eternity. Trust the Shepherd.

—Your Thoughts for Today—

THE ANCHOR HOLDS

*We have this hope—like a sure and firm anchor of the soul—
that enters the inner sanctuary behind the curtain.*

Hebrews 6:19 Holman CSB

Corrie ten Boom observed, "In order to realize the worth of the anchor, we need to feel the stress of the storm." And she was right. In the storms of life, we come to realize that God is the immovable anchor that keeps us safe and steady.

As you make the journey through cancer and beyond it, remember that God is your Protector. He is with you always, and He is trustworthy. He cannot be moved, and when you join your heart to His, you cannot be moved, either.

———

Through all of the crises of life—and we all are going to experience them—we have this magnificent Anchor.

Franklin Graham

—Your Thoughts for Today—

_____

_____

_____

_____

_____

_____

_____

NEED COURAGE? GOD CAN HANDLE IT

Do not be afraid or discouraged, for the LORD is the one who goes before you. He will be with you; he will neither fail you nor forsake you.

Deuteronomy 31:8 NLT

During our darkest moments, God offers us courage and strength if we turn our hearts and our prayers to Him.

As believing Christians, we have every reason to live courageously. After all, the ultimate battle has already been fought and won on the cross at Calvary. But sometimes, because we are imperfect human beings who possess imperfect faith, we fall prey to fear and doubt. The answer to our fears, of course, is God.

The next time you find your courage tested to the limit, remember that God is as near as your next breath. Call upon Him in your hour of need and then be comforted. Whatever your challenge, whatever your trouble, God can handle it . . . and will!

—Your Thoughts for Today—

FAITH THAT MOVES MOUNTAINS

I assure you: If anyone says to this mountain, "Be lifted up and thrown into the sea," and does not doubt in his heart, but believes that what he says will happen, it will be done for him.
Mark 11:23 Holman CSB

All of us have mountains to climb and mountains to move. Moving those mountains requires faith.

Are you a mountain-mover whose faith is evident for all to see? Hopefully so. God needs more men who are willing to move mountains for His glory and for His kingdom.

God walks with you through your illness and your recovery; He's ready and willing to strengthen you. Accept His strength today. And remember—Jesus taught His disciples that if they had faith, they could move mountains. You can too . . . so with no further ado, let the mountain-moving begin.

Only God can move mountains, but faith and prayer can move God.

E. M. Bounds

—Your Thoughts for Today—

_____

_____

_____

_____

_____

THE ULTIMATE TRAVELING COMPANION

The LORD is my rock, and my fortress, and my deliverer; my God, my strength, in whom I will trust....

Psalm 18:2 KJV

As you take the next step in your journey beyond cancer, are you willing to enlist God as your traveling companion? Are you willing to trust Him, to obey Him, to honor Him, and to love Him? And are you willing to consult Him before you make important decisions, not after? Hopefully, you can answer these questions with a resounding yes.

Today, as a gift to yourself and your loved ones, summon the courage to follow God. Even if the path seems difficult, even if your heart is fearful, trust your Heavenly Father and follow Him. Trust Him with your day, with your healing, and with your life. Let Him guide your steps. He will not lead you astray.

———

Faith does not eliminate problems. Faith keeps you in a trusting relationship with God in the midst of your problems.

Henry Blackaby

—Your Thoughts for Today—

A WALK WITH GOD

For I have given you an example that you also should do just as I have done for you.

John 13:15 Holman CSB

Each day, we are confronted with countless opportunities to serve God and to follow in the footsteps of His Son. When we do, our Heavenly Father guides our steps and blesses our endeavors. As citizens of a fast-changing world, we face challenges that sometimes leave us feeling overworked, overcommitted, and overwhelmed. But God has different plans for us. He intends that we slow down long enough to praise Him and to glorify His Son. When we do, He lifts our spirits and enriches our lives.

Today provides a glorious opportunity to place yourself in the service of the One who is the Giver of all blessings. May you seek His will, may you trust His Word, and may you walk in the footsteps of His Son.

I have a great need for Christ; I have a great Christ for my need.

C. H. Spurgeon

—Your Thoughts for Today—

_____

_____

_____

_____

_____

HE IS SHAPING US

Yet Lord, You are our Father; we are the clay, and You are our potter; we all are the work of Your hands.

Isaiah 64:8 Holman CSB

God has made this promise to you: He will instruct you in the way you should go. God is always willing to teach, and you should always be willing to learn . . . but sometimes, you will be tempted to ignore God's instruction. Don't do it—instead of ignoring God, start praying about your situation . . . and start listening!

When we sincerely offer heartfelt prayers to our Heavenly Father, He will give direction and meaning to our lives—but He won't force us to follow Him. To the contrary, God has given us the free will to follow His commandments . . . or not.

When we genuinely and humbly seek His instruction, God touches our hearts and leads us on the path of His choosing. It's the proper path for all mankind, and it's the right path for you. Follow it today.

The Word of God, prayer, and suffering are the three "tools" that God uses in our lives.

Warren Wiersbe

—Your Thoughts for Today—

_____

_____

_____

_____

THE FUTURE IS IN HIS HANDS

*The earth and everything in it, the world and its inhabitants,
belong to the Lord.*

Psalm 24:1 Holman CSB

The old saying is both familiar and true: "Man proposes and God disposes." Our world unfolds according to God's plans, not our wishes. Thus, the future belongs to God, and we must acknowledge His sovereignty over all things.

Are you planning for a better tomorrow for yourself and your family? If so, you are to be congratulated: God rewards forethought in the same way that He often punishes impulsiveness. But as you make your plans, do so with humility, with gratitude, and with trust in your Heavenly Father. His hand directs the future, and because eternity belongs to Him, you are protected now and forever.

That we may not complain of what is, let us see God's hand in all events; and, that we may not be afraid of what shall be, let us see all events in God's hand.

Matthew Henry

—Your Thoughts for Today—

HIS RIGHTFUL PLACE

You shall have no other gods before Me.

Exodus 20:3 NKJV

When Jesus was tempted by Satan, the Master's response was unambiguous. Jesus chose to worship the Lord and serve Him only. We, as followers of Christ, must follow in His footsteps by placing God first.

When we place God in a position of secondary importance, we do ourselves great harm. When we allow temptations or distractions to come between us and our Creator, we suffer. But, when we imitate Jesus and place the Lord in His rightful place—at the center of our lives—then we claim spiritual treasures that will endure forever.

Give God what's right—not what's left!

Anonymous

—Your Thoughts for Today—

NO COMPLAINTS

Don't criticize one another, brothers.

James 4:11 Holman CSB

When you're feeling sick or worried, you may find it easy to complain about any number of frustrations, some great, some small. But if you allow yourself to fall into the trap of negativity, you'll only increase your suffering. Habitual griping can be a serious roadblock on your path to spiritual abundance and earthly peace.

Sometime today, you may be tempted to complain about some aspect of your treatment. Don't do it! Instead, make it a practice to count your blessings, not your hardships. It's the decent way to live and the best way to heal.

I am sure it is never sadness—a proper, straight, natural response to loss—that does people harm, but all the other things, all the resentment, dismay, doubt and self-pity with which it is usually complicated.

C. S. Lewis

—Your Thoughts for Today—

_____

_____

_____

_____

_____

_____

YOUR TRAVELING COMPANION

But thanks be to God, who gives us the victory through our Lord Jesus Christ. Therefore, my beloved brethren, be steadfast, immovable, always abounding in the work of the Lord, knowing that your labor is not in vain in the Lord.

1 Corinthians 15:57-58 NKJV

As you continue to seek God's purpose for your life, you will undoubtedly experience your fair share of disappointments, detours, false starts, and failures. When you do, don't become discouraged: God's not finished with you yet.

The old saying is as true today as it was when it was first spoken: "Life is a marathon, not a sprint." That's why wise travelers select a traveling companion who never tires and never falters. That partner, of course, is your Heavenly Father. So pray as if everything depended upon God, and work as if everything depended upon you. And trust God to do the rest.

Perseverance is more than endurance. It is endurance combined with absolute assurance and certainty that what we are looking for is going to happen.

Oswald Chambers

—Your Thoughts for Today—

GROWTH THROUGH ADVERSITY

I will show you what someone is like who comes to Me, hears My words, and acts on them: He is like a man building a house, who dug deep and laid the foundation on the rock. When the flood rose, the river crashed against that house and couldn't shake it, because it was well built.

Luke 6:47-48 Holman CSB

Many of life's most important lessons are painful to learn. During times of heartbreak and hardship, we must be courageous and we must be patient, knowing that in His own time, God will reveal His plans if we invite Him into our hearts. In those quiet moments when we open our hearts to God, the One who made us keeps remaking us. He gives us direction, perspective, wisdom, and courage.

When it comes to your faith, God doesn't intend for you to become "fully grown," at least not in this lifetime. In fact, God still has important lessons that He intends to teach you. So ask yourself this: what lesson is God trying to teach me today? And then go about the business of learning it.

—Your Thoughts for Today—

_____

_____

_____

_____

_____

TESTED

God's solid foundation stands firm.

2 Timothy 2:19 Holman CSB

Are you being tested? Is your faith being shaken to its very foundation? Is your vision of the future clouded? If so, it's time to turn your concerns over to God in prayer. And, it's time to find someone you can talk to. And perhaps it's time to reconsider the lessons that you are learning every day about yourself, about your faith, and about your Creator.

Corrie ten Boom observed, "God makes the sunshine every day, even though it is sometimes hidden behind the clouds." If the clouds have temporarily hidden the sun from view, keep your eyes and your heart open. God is not just near; He is here. And, He can help you overcome every hardship and pass every test, today, tomorrow, and forever.

———

Faith is always tested for three reasons: to prove whether our faith is real; to help our faith grow; and to bring glory to the Lord.

Warren Wiersbe

—Your Thoughts for Today—

_____

_____

_____

_____

_____

THANKSGIVING YES . . .
SELF-PITY, NO

Stop your anger! Turn from your rage! Do not envy others—it only leads to harm.

Psalm 37:8 NLT

Charles Swindoll advises, "When you're on the verge of throwing a pity party thanks to your despairing thoughts, go back to the Word of God." How true. Self-pity is not only an unproductive way to think, it is also an affront to your Father in heaven. God's Word promises that His children can receive abundance, peace, love, and eternal life. These gifts are not earned; they are an outpouring from God, a manifestation of His grace. With these rich blessings, how can we, as believers, feel sorry for ourselves?

Self-pity and peace cannot coexist in the same mind. Bitterness and joy cannot coexist in the same heart. Thanksgiving and despair are mutually exclusive. So, if your unreliable thoughts are allowing despair and worry to dominate your life, train yourself to think less about your troubles and more about God's blessings. Focus your mind on Him, and let your worries fend for themselves.

—Your Thoughts for Today—

_____

_____

_____

_____

FINDING HOPE

These things I have spoken to you, that in Me you may have peace. In the world you will have tribulation; but be of good cheer, I have overcome the world.

John 16:33 NKJV

There are few sadder sights on earth than the sight of a person who has lost all hope. In difficult times, hope can be elusive, but Christians need never lose it. After all, God is good; His love endures; He has promised His children the gift of eternal life.

If you find yourself falling into the spiritual traps of worry and discouragement, consider the words of Jesus. It was Christ who promised that He would overcome the world. This world is indeed a place of trials and tribulations, but as believers, we are secure. God has promised us peace, joy, and eternal life. And, of course, God always keeps His promises.

———

Troubles we bear trustfully can bring us a fresh vision of God and a new outlook on life, an outlook of peace and hope.

Billy Graham

—Your Thoughts for Today—

_____

_____

_____

_____

_____

LIFE ABUNDANT

I have come that they may have life, and that they may have it more abundantly.

John 10:10 NKJV

The 10th chapter of John tells us that Christ came to earth so that our lives might be filled with abundance. But what, exactly, did Jesus mean when He promised "life...more abundantly"? Was He referring to material possessions, or fame, or wealth, or health? Hardly. Jesus offers a different kind of abundance: a spiritual richness that extends beyond the temporal boundaries of this world. This everlasting abundance is available to all who seek it and claim it. May we, as believers, claim the riches of Christ Jesus every day that we live, and may we share His blessings with all who cross our path.

The only way you can experience abundant life is to surrender your plans to Him.

Charles Stanley

—Your Thoughts for Today—

ACCEPTING GOD'S GIFT

For God loved the world in this way: He gave His only Son,
so that everyone who believes in Him will not perish but have
eternal life.

John 3:16 Holman CSB

G od loves you—His love for you is deeper and more profound than you can imagine. God's love for you is so great that He sent His only Son to this earth to die for your sins and to offer you the priceless gift of eternal life.

You must decide whether or not to accept God's gift. Will you ignore it or embrace it? Will you return it or neglect it? Will you invite Christ to dwell in the center of your heart, or will you relegate Him to a position of lesser importance? The decision is yours, and so are the consequences. So choose wisely . . . and choose today.

Ask Christ to come into your heart to forgive you and help you. When you do, Christ will take up residence in your life by His Holy Spirit, and when you face temptations and trials, you will no longer face them alone.

Billy Graham

—Your Thoughts for Today—

_____

_____

_____

_____

_____

WHERE IS GOD LEADING?

Consider it a great joy, my brothers, whenever you experience various trials, knowing that the testing of your faith produces endurance. But endurance must do its complete work, so that you may be mature and complete, lacking nothing.

James 1:2-4 Holman CSB

Whether we realize it or not, times of adversity can be times of intense personal and spiritual growth. Our difficult days are also times when we can learn and relearn some of life's most important lessons.

The next time you experience a difficult moment, a difficult day, or a difficult year, ask yourself this question: Where is God leading me? In times of struggle and sorrow, you can be certain that God is leading you to a place of His choosing. Your duty is to watch, to pray, to listen, and to follow.

Even in the winter, even in the midst of the storm, the sun is still there. Somewhere, up above the clouds, it still shines and warms and pulls at the life buried deep inside the brown branches and frozen earth. The sun is there! Spring will come.

Gloria Gaither

—Your Thoughts for Today—

_____

_____

_____

_____

THIS IS HIS DAY

This is the day the LORD has made. We will rejoice and be glad in it.

Psalm 118:24 NLT

The 118th Psalm reminds us that today, like every other day, is a cause for celebration. But on the days when we're feeling sick or discouraged, we may not feel like celebrating. But even during tough times, we have many reasons to celebrate.

Today is a non-renewable resource—once it's gone, it's gone forever. Our responsibility, of course, is to use this day in the service of God's will and according to His commandments.

Today, treasure the time that God has given you. Give Him the glory and the praise and the thanksgiving that He deserves. And search for the hidden possibilities that God has placed along your path. This day is a priceless gift from above, so use it wisely and encourage others to do likewise.

I choose joy. I will refuse the temptation to be cynical; cynicism is the tool of a lazy thinker. I will refuse to see people as anything less than human beings, created by God. I will refuse to see any problem as anything less than an opportunity to see God.

Max Lucado

—Your Thoughts for Today—

_____

_____

_____

DEALING WITH DISAPPOINTMENT

For we do not want you to be ignorant, brethren, of our trouble which came to us in Asia: that we were burdened beyond measure, above strength, so that we despaired even of life. Yes, we had the sentence of death in ourselves, that we should not trust in ourselves but in God who raises the dead, who delivered us from so great a death, and does deliver us; in whom we trust that He will still deliver us.

2 Corinthians 1:8-10 NKJV

From time to time, all of us face life-altering disappointments that leave us breathless. Oftentimes, these disappointments come unexpectedly, leaving us with more questions than answers. But even when we don't have all the answers—or, for that matter, even when we don't seem to have any of the answers—God does. Whatever our circumstances, whether we stand atop the highest mountain or wander through the darkest valley, God is ready to protect us, to comfort us, and to heal us. Our task is to let Him.

The Christian life is not a constant high. I have my moments of deep discouragement. I have to go to God in prayer with tears in my eyes, and say, "O God, forgive me," or "Help me."

Billy Graham

—Your Thoughts for Today—

_____

_____

_____

RESTORING YOUR STRENGTH

Therefore, this is what the Lord says: If you return, I will restore you; you will stand in My presence.

Jeremiah 15:19 Holman CSB

Even if you're an inspired believer, even if you're normally upbeat about your future and your life, you may, on occasion, find yourself running on empty. Worries about health can drain your strength and rob you of the joy that is rightfully yours in Christ. When you are tired, discouraged, or despondent, there is a source from which you can draw the power needed to recharge your spiritual batteries. That source is God.

Are you tired or troubled? Turn your heart toward God in prayer. Are you weak or worried? Take the time—or, more accurately, make the time—to delve deeply into God's Holy Word. Are you spiritually depleted? Call upon fellow believers to support you, and call upon Christ to renew your spirit and your life. When you do, you'll discover that, in time, the Creator of the universe will deliver you from sorrow and place a new song on your lips.

Walking with God leads to receiving his intimate counsel, and counseling leads to deep restoration.

John Eldredge

—Your Thoughts for Today—

_____

_____

_____

TAKING UP THE CROSS

Then He said to them all, "If anyone wants to come with Me, he must deny himself, take up his cross daily, and follow Me."

Luke 9:23 Holman CSB

When we have been saved by Christ, we can, if we choose, become passive Christians. We can sit back, secure in our own salvation, and let other believers spread the healing message of Jesus. But to do so is wrong. Instead, we are commanded to become disciples of the One who has saved us, and to do otherwise is a sin of omission with terrible consequences.

When Jesus addressed His disciples, He warned them that each one must, "take up his cross daily and follow me" (Luke 9:23 NIV). Christ's message was clear: in order to follow Him, Christ's disciples must deny themselves and, instead, trust Him completely. Nothing has changed since then.

Do you seek to fulfill God's purpose for your life? Then follow Christ. Follow Him by picking up His cross today and every day that you live. Then, you will quickly discover that Christ's love has the power to change everything, including you.

—Your Thoughts for Today—

_____

_____

_____

TODAY'S OPPORTUNITIES

*But encourage each other daily, while it is still called today,
so that none of you is hardened by sin's deception.*

Hebrews 3:13 Holman CSB

The 118th Psalm reminds us, "This is the day which the Lord hath made; we will rejoice and be glad in it" (v. 24 KJV). As we rejoice in this day that the Lord has given us, let us remember that an important part of today's celebration is the time we spend celebrating others. Each day provides countless opportunities to encourage others and to praise their good works. When we do, we not only spread seeds of joy and happiness, we also follow the commandments of God's Holy Word.

How can we build others up? By celebrating their victories and their accomplishments. So look for the good in others and celebrate the good that you find. When you do, you'll be a powerful force of encouragement in the world…and a worthy servant to your God.

A lot of people have gone further than they thought they could because someone else thought they could.

Zig Ziglar

—Your Thoughts for Today—

_____

_____

_____

_____

_____

HONORING GOD

Honor the Lord with your possessions, and with the firstfruits of all your increase; so your barns will be filled with plenty.

Proverbs 3:9-10 NKJV

Whom will you choose to honor today? If you honor God and place Him at the center of your life, every day is a cause for celebration. At times, your life is probably hectic, demanding, and complicated. When the demands of life leave you rushing from place to place with scarcely a moment to spare, you may fail to pause and thank your Creator for the blessings He has bestowed upon you. But that's a big mistake. So, whatever your circumstances, honor God for who He is and for what He has done for you. And don't just honor Him on Sunday morning. Praise Him all day long, every day, for as long as you live . . . and then for all eternity.

Praise opens the window of our hearts, preparing us to walk more closely with God. Prayer raises the window of our spirit, enabling us to listen more clearly to the Father.

Max Lucado

—Your Thoughts for Today—

_____

_____

_____

_____

_____

FEEDING THE CHURCH

The church, you see, is not peripheral to the world; the world is peripheral to the church. The church is Christ's body, in which he speaks and acts, by which he fills everything with his presence.

Ephesians 1:23 MSG

In the Book of Acts, Luke reminds us to "feed the church of God" (20:28). As Christians who have been saved by a loving, compassionate Creator, we are compelled not only to worship Him in our hearts but also to worship Him in the presence of fellow believers.

Do you feed the church of God? The answer to this question will have a profound impact on the quality and direction of your spiritual journey.

So don't let illness separate you from your church. Don't just go to church out of habit. Go to church out of a sincere desire to know and worship God. When you do, you'll be blessed by the One who sent His Son to die so that you might have everlasting life.

And how can we improve the church? Simply and only by improving ourselves.

A. W. Tozer

—Your Thoughts for Today—

THE VOICE INSIDE YOUR HEAD

Trust God from the bottom of your heart; don't try to figure out everything on your own. Listen for God's voice in everything you do, everywhere you go; he's the one who will keep you on track.

Proverbs 3:5-6 MSG

As you make the journey through cancer and beyond, you'll probably have choices to make . . . lots of choices. Whenever you're about to make an important decision, be still and listen carefully to the quiet voice inside. Sometimes, of course, it's tempting to do otherwise. From time to time you'll be tempted to abandon your better judgment by ignoring your conscience. But remember: a conscience is a terrible thing to waste. So instead of ignoring that quiet little voice, pay careful attention to it. If you do, your conscience will lead you in the right direction—in fact, it's trying to lead you right now. So listen . . . and learn.

God has revealed Himself in man's conscience. Conscience has been described as the light of the soul.

Billy Graham

—Your Thoughts for Today—

THE STORMS OF LIFE

Immediately Jesus spoke to them. "Have courage! It is I. Don't be afraid."

Matthew 14:27 Holman CSB

A storm rose quickly on the Sea of Galilee, and the disciples were afraid. Although they had seen Jesus perform many miracles, the disciples feared for their lives, so they turned to their Savior, and He calmed the waters and the wind.

Sometimes, we, like the disciples, feel threatened by the inevitable storms of life. And when we are fearful, we, too, can turn to Christ for courage and for comfort.

As you make the journey through cancer and beyond it, you may find yourself struggling with worries, or fears, or both. The next time you're afraid, remember that the One who calmed the wind and the waves is also your personal Savior. And remember that the ultimate battle has already been won at Calvary. Whatever your circumstances, you can live courageously in the promises of your Lord...and you should.

Down through the centuries, in times of trouble and trial, God has brought courage to the hearts of those who love Him. The Bible is filled with assurances of God's help and comfort in every kind of trouble.

Billy Graham

There are four essentials for victory in trials: a joyful attitude, an understanding mind, a surrendered will, and a heart that wants to believe.

Warren Wiersbe

We all go through pain and sorrow, but the presence of God, like a warm, comforting blanket, can shield us and protect us, and allow the deep inner joy to surface, even in the most devastating circumstances.

Barbara Johnson

The fear of God is the death of every other fear.

C. H. Spurgeon

Christians are like tea bags. It's only when they get into hot water that you find out how strong they are.

Anonymous

How do you walk in faith? By claiming the promises of God and obeying the Word of God, in spite of what you see, how you feel, or what may happen.

Warren Wiersbe

—Your Thoughts for Today—

_____

_____

_____

_____

_____

_____

_____

_____

_____

_____

CHRIST'S LOVE CHANGES EVERYTHING

*Your old life is dead. Your new life, which is your real life—
even though invisible to spectators—is with Christ in God.
He is your life.*

Colossians 3:3 MSG

What does the love of Christ mean to His believers? It changes everything. His love is perfect and steadfast. Even though we are fallible, and wayward, the Good Shepherd cares for us still. Even though we have fallen far short of the Father's commandments, Christ loves us with a power and depth that is beyond our understanding. And, as we accept Christ's love and walk in Christ's footsteps, our lives bear testimony to His power and to His grace. Yes, Christ's love changes everything; may we invite Him into our hearts so it can then change everything in us.

There is not a single thing that Jesus cannot change, control, and conquer because He is the living Lord.

Franklin Graham

—Your Thoughts for Today—

_____

_____

_____

_____

_____

_____

HIS AWESOME CREATION

And to every beast of the earth and to every bird of the sky
and to every thing that moves on the earth which has life . . .
God saw all that He had made, and behold, it was very good.

Genesis 1:30-31 NASB

When we consider God's glorious universe, we marvel at the miracle of nature. The smallest seedlings and grandest stars are all part of God's infinite creation. God has placed His handiwork on display for all to see, and if we are wise, we will make time each day to celebrate the world that surrounds us.

Today, as you continue your journey towards healing, pause to consider the majesty of heaven and earth. It is as miraculous as it is beautiful, as incomprehensible as it is breathtaking.

The Psalmist reminds us that the heavens are a declaration of God's glory (Psalm 19:1). May we never cease to praise the Father for a universe that stands as an awesome testimony to His presence and His power.

Today you will encounter God's creation. When you see the beauty around you, let each detail remind you to lift your head in praise.

Max Lucado

—Your Thoughts for Today—

YOU ARE BLESSED

I will make them and the area around My hill a blessing: I will send down showers in their season—showers of blessing.
Ezekiel 34:26 Holman CSB

I f you sat down and began counting your blessings, how long would it take? The answer to that question is: a very, long time, indeed. Your blessings include life, freedom, family, friends, talents, and possessions, for starters. But, your greatest blessing—a gift that is yours for the asking—is God's gift of salvation through Christ Jesus.

Today, refuse to give in the sin of self-pity. Instead, begin making a list of your blessings. You most certainly will not be able to make a complete list of God's gifts, but take a few moments and jot down as many blessings as you can. Then give thanks to the Giver of all good things. His love for you is eternal, as are His gifts. And it's never too soon—or too late—to offer Him thanks.

God's kindness is not like the sunset—brilliant in its intensity, but dying every second. God's generosity keeps coming and coming and coming.

Bill Hybels

—Your Thoughts for Today—

_____

_____

_____

_____

_____

EXPERIENCING HIS PEACE

Peace I leave with you. My peace I give to you. I do not give to you as the world gives. Your heart must not be troubled or fearful.

John 14:27 Holman CSB

Have you found the genuine peace that can be yours through Jesus Christ? The beautiful words of John 14:27 remind us that Jesus offers us peace, not as the world gives, but as He alone gives. Our challenge is to accept Christ's peace into our hearts and then, as best we can, to share His peace with our neighbors.

Today, as a gift to yourself, to your family, and to your friends, claim the inner peace that is your spiritual birthright: the peace of Jesus Christ. It is offered freely; it has been paid for in full; it is yours for the asking. So ask. And then share.

God's peace is like a river, not a pond. In other words, a sense of health and well-being, both of which are expressions of the Hebrew shalom, can permeate our homes even when we're in white-water rapids.

Beth Moore

—Your Thoughts for Today—

_____

_____

_____

_____

_____

DAILY VICTORY

Lord, I turn my hope to You. My God, I trust in You.
Psalm 25:1-2 Holman CSB

For Christians, every day begins and ends with God and His Son. Christ came to this earth to give us abundant life and eternal salvation. We give thanks to our Maker when we treasure each day and use it to the fullest.

Even if you're struggling with a serious illness, even if you're feeling very sick or very sad, you can still do things to improve your life and honor your Creator. So no matter what this day brings, dedicate it to God. When you do, you'll discover that you and the Father, working together, can do infinitely more than you can do by yourself.

The truth is that even in the midst of trouble, happy moments swim by us every day, like shining fish waiting to be caught.

Barbara Johnson

—Your Thoughts for Today—

THE NEED FOR SELF-DISCIPLINE

Do you not know that the runners in a stadium all race, but only one receives the prize? Run in such a way that you may win. Now everyone who competes exercises self-control in everything. However, they do it to receive a perishable crown, but we an imperishable one.

1 Corinthians 9:24-25 Holman CSB

Nobody needs to tell you that fighting cancer is very difficult indeed. So, the journey through and beyond your illness requires discipline.

Vance Havner observed, "The alternative to discipline is disaster." And he was right. In life, the greatest rewards seldom fall into our laps. Usually, victory results from hard work and perseverance. May we, as disciplined believers, be willing to work for the rewards we so earnestly desire.

Wouldn't it make astounding difference, not only in the quality of the work we do, but also in the satisfaction, even our joy, if we recognized God's gracious gift in every single task?

Elisabeth Elliot

—Your Thoughts for Today—

_____

_____

_____

_____

_____

HIS PROMISES

Let us hold on to the confession of our hope without wavering, for He who promised is faithful.

Hebrews 10:23 Holman CSB

The Christian faith is founded upon promises that are contained in a unique book. That book is the Holy Bible. The Bible is a roadmap for life here on earth and for life eternal. As Christians, we are called upon to study its meaning, to trust its promises, to follow its commandments, and to share its Good News. God's Holy Word is, indeed, a transforming, life-changing, one-of-a-kind treasure. And, a passing acquaintance with the Good Book is insufficient for Christians who seek to obey God's Word and understand His will.

God has made promises to you, and He intends to keep them. So take God at His word: trust His promises and share them with your family, with your friends, and with the world.

There are four words I wish we would never forget, and they are, "God keeps his word."

Charles Swindoll

—Your Thoughts for Today—

RICHLY BLESSED

Each person should do as he has decided in his heart—not out of regret or out of necessity, for God loves a cheerful giver.

2 Corinthians 9:7 Holman CSB

God's Word commands us to be generous, compassionate servants to those who need our support. As believers, we have been richly blessed by our Creator. We, in turn, are called to share our gifts, our possessions, our testimonies, and our talents.

The theme of generosity is one of the cornerstones of Christ's teachings. If we are to be disciples of Christ, we, too, must be cheerful, generous, courageous givers. Our Savior expects no less from us. And He deserves no less.

———

Giving to God and, in His name, to others, is not something that we do; it the result of what we are.

Warren Wiersbe

—Your Thoughts for Today—

_____

_____

_____

_____

_____

_____

_____

THE GIFT OF SALVATION

For by grace you are saved through faith, and this is not from yourselves; it is God's gift—not from works, so that no one can boast.

Ephesians 2:8-9 Holman CSB

God has given us so many gifts, but none can compare with the gift of salvation. We have not earned our salvation; it is a gift from God. When we accept Christ into our hearts, we are saved by His grace.

God's grace is the ultimate gift, and we owe to Him the ultimate in thanksgiving. Let us praise the Creator for His priceless gift, and let us share the Good News with all who cross our paths. We return our Father's love by accepting His grace and by sharing His message and His love. When we do, we are eternally blessed . . . and the Father smiles.

The grace of God is infinite and eternal. As it had no beginning, so it can have no end, and being an attribute of God, it is as boundless as infinitude.

A. W. Tozer

—Your Thoughts for Today—

_____

_____

_____

_____

_____

SENSING HIS PRESENCE

Where can I go from Your Spirit? Or where can I flee from Your presence? If I ascend into heaven, You are there; If I make my bed in hell, behold, You are there. If I take the wings of the morning, and dwell in the uttermost parts of the sea, Even there Your hand shall lead me, and Your right hand shall hold me.

Psalm 139:7-10 NKJV

I f God is everywhere, why does He sometimes seem so far away? The answer to that question, of course, has nothing to do with God and everything to do with us.

When we begin each day on our knees, in praise and worship to Him, God often seems very near indeed. But, if we ignore God's presence or—worse yet—rebel against it altogether, the world in which we live becomes a spiritual wasteland.

Today, and every day hereafter, thank God and praise Him. He is the Giver of all things good. Wherever you are, whether you are happy or sad, victorious or vanquished, celebrate God's presence. And be comforted. For He is here.

—Your Thoughts for Today—

LIVE AND LOVE

He said to him, "You shall love the Lord your God with all your heart, with all your soul, and with all your mind. This is the greatest and most important commandment."

Matthew 22:37-38 Holman CSB

Christ's words are clear: we are to love God first, and secondly, we are to love others as we love ourselves. These two commands are seldom easy, and because we are imperfect beings, we often fall short. But God's Holy Word commands us to try.

The Christian path is an exercise in love and forgiveness. If we are to walk in Christ's footsteps, we must forgive those who have done us harm, and we must accept Christ's love by sharing it freely with family, friends, neighbors, and strangers.

———

The Christian life has two different dimensions: faith toward God and love toward men. You cannot separate the two.

Warren Wiersbe

—Your Thoughts for Today—

_____

_____

_____

_____

_____

_____

YOUR SPIRITUAL GIFTS

I remind you to keep ablaze the gift of God that is in you.
2 Timothy 1:6 Holman CSB

Have you given much thought to your spiritual gifts? Whether you realize it or not, you have a surprising array of God-given talents that you can use to honor Him and serve His kingdom here on earth.

How will you use your spiritual gifts? Will you humbly ask God to use you as an instrument of His will, and will you prayerfully ask Him to use your talents for His glory and His purposes? If you do, God has promised to guide your steps and answer your prayers.

So today, ask God to use all your talents—spiritual and otherwise—to improve His world and yours. When you do, God will use you and bless you, starting now and ending never.

God is the giver, and we are the receivers. And His richest gifts are bestowed not upon those who do the greatest things, but upon those who accept His abundance and His grace.

Hannah Whitall Smith

—Your Thoughts for Today—

THE CLASSROOM

Don't abandon wisdom, and she will watch over you; love her, and she will guard you.

Proverbs 4:6 Holman CSB

L ife is a grand and glorious classroom; school is always in session; and the rest is up to us. Every day provides opportunities to learn, to grow, and to share our wisdom with the world.

Sometimes, God sends lessons disguised as problems. Sometimes He wraps His messages inside pain, or loss, or struggle, or exhaustion. But no matter our circumstances, the Father never stops teaching. And if we're wise, we never stop looking for His lessons.

When it comes to your faith, God doesn't intend for you to stand still. He wants you to keep learning and growing every day of your life. No matter how "grown-up" you may be, you still have growing to do. And the more you grow, the more beautiful you become, inside and out.

Since adversity is God's most effective tool insofar as spiritual growth is concerned, the degree to which we desire to grow spiritually corresponds to our ability to handle adversity successfully.

Charles Stanley

—Your Thoughts for Today—

_____

_____

_____

HE DOESN'T CHANGE

For unto us a Child is born, unto us a Son is given; and the government will be upon His shoulder. And His name will be called Wonderful, Counselor, Mighty God, Everlasting Father, Prince of Peace.

Isaiah 9:6 NKJV

Are you facing a troubling diagnosis, or difficult circumstances, or unwelcome changes? If so, please remember that God is far bigger than any problem you may face. So, instead of worrying about life's inevitable challenges, put your faith in the Father and His only begotten Son: "Jesus Christ is the same yesterday, today, and forever" (Hebrews 13:8 NKJV). And remember: it is precisely because your Savior does not change that you can face your challenges with courage for today and hope for tomorrow.

———

Conditions are always changing; therefore, I must not be dependent upon conditions. What matters supremely is my soul and my relationship to God.

Corrie ten Boom

—Your Thoughts for Today—

BEYOND THE PAIN

The Lord is near to those who have a broken heart.

Psalm 34:18 NKJV

It's an age-old riddle: Why does God allow us to suffer? After all, since we trust that God is all-powerful, and since we trust that His hand shapes our lives, why doesn't He simply rescue us—and our loved ones—from all hardship and pain?

God's Word teaches us again and again that He loves us and wants the best for us. And the Bible also teaches us that God is ever-present and always watchful. So why, we wonder, if God is really so concerned with every detail of our lives, does He permit us to endure emotions like grief, sadness, shame, or fear? And why does He allow tragic circumstances to invade the lives of good people? These questions perplex us, especially when our losses are staggering.

On occasion, all of us must endure life-changing personal losses that leave us breathless. When we pass through the dark valleys of life, we often ask, "Why me?" We wonder, again and again, why God permits us to suffer.

Even when we cannot understand God's plans, we must trust them. And even when we are impatient for healing to begin, we must trust God's timing. If we seek to live in accordance with His plan for our lives, we must continue to study His Word, and we must be watchful for His signs, knowing that in time, He will lead us through the valleys, onward to the mountaintop.

Pain is the fuel of passion—it energizes us with an intensity to change that we don't normally possess.

Rick Warren

When you suffer and lose, that does not mean you are being disobedient to God. In fact, it might mean you're right in the center of His will. The path of obedience is often marked by times of suffering and loss.

Charles Swindoll

Suffering will be either your master or your servant, depending on how you handle the crises of life.

Warren Wiersbe

O Lord, thank You that Your side of the embroidery of our life is always perfect. That is such a comfort when our side is sometimes so mixed up.

Corrie ten Boom

—Your Thoughts for Today—

_____

_____

_____

_____

_____

_____

_____

_____

THE POWER OF WORDS

The wise store up knowledge, but the mouth of the fool hastens destruction.

Proverbs 10:14 Holman CSB

All too often, in the rush to have ourselves heard, we speak first and think next…with unfortunate results. God's Word reminds us that, "Reckless words pierce like a sword, but the tongue of the wise brings healing" (Proverbs 12:18 NIV). If we seek to be a source of encouragement to friends and family, then we must measure our words carefully. Words are important: they can hurt or heal. Words can uplift us or discourage us, and reckless words, spoken in haste, cannot be erased.

Today, measure your words carefully. Use words of kindness and praise, not words of anger or derision. Remember that you have the power to heal others or to injure them, to lift others up or to hold them back. When you lift them up, your wisdom will bring healing and comfort to a world that needs both.

————

Attitude and the spirit in which we communicate are as important as the words we say.

Charles Stanley

—Your Thoughts for Today—

GOD'S GUIDANCE
AND YOUR PATH

Trust in the LORD with all your heart; do not depend on your own understanding. Seek his will in all you do, and he will direct your paths.

Proverbs 3:5-6 NLT

Proverbs 3:5-6 makes this promise: if you acknowledge God's sovereignty over every aspect of your life, He will guide your path. And, as you prayerfully consider the path that God intends for you to take, here are things you should do: You should study His Word and be ever-watchful for His signs. You should associate with fellow believers who will encourage your spiritual growth. You should listen carefully to that inner voice that speaks to you in the quiet moments of your daily devotionals. And you should be patient. Your Heavenly Father may not always reveal Himself as quickly as you would like, but rest assured that God intends to use you in powerful, unexpected ways. Your challenge is to watch, to listen, to learn . . . and to follow.

Only by walking with God can we hope to find the path that leads to life.

John Eldredge

—Your Thoughts for Today—

_____

_____

_____

_____

WORSHIP HIM EVERY DAY

Worship the Lord your God and . . . serve Him only.

Matthew 4:10 Holman CSB

While you're healing, regular worship can have a profound impact on your recovery. If you worship God sincerely and often, you'll be blessed by the time you spend with the Creator. But if your pain causes you to withdraw from your church, or from God, you'll be doing yourself a severe disservice.

As you journey through and beyond cancer, be sure to worship God seven days a week, not just on Sundays. Start each day with a time of prayer and meditation. Then, throughout the day, talk to God often. When you do, He will strengthen your spirit and guide your steps.

When God is at the center of your life, you worship. When he's not, you worry.

Rick Warren

—Your Thoughts for Today—

_____

_____

_____

_____

_____

_____

_____

_____

THE SHEPHERD'S GIFT

My cup runs over. Surely goodness and mercy shall follow me all the days of my life; and I will dwell in the house of the Lord forever.

Psalm 23:5-6 NKJV

The Word of God is clear: Christ came in order that we might have life abundant and life eternal. Eternal life is priceless possession of all who invite Christ into their hearts, but God's abundance is optional: He does not force it upon us.

When we entrust our hearts and our days to the One who created us, we experience abundance through the grace and sacrifice of His Son. But, when we turn our thoughts and direct our energies away from God's commandments, we inevitably forfeit the spiritual abundance that might otherwise be ours.

Do you sincerely seek the riches that our Savior offers to those who give themselves to Him? Then follow Him completely and obey Him without reservation. When you do, you will receive the love and the abundance that He has promised.

God loves you and wants you to experience peace and life—abundant and eternal.

Billy Graham

—Your Thoughts for Today—

_____

_____

_____

BEYOND ADVERSITY

*I will be with you when you pass through the waters . . .
when you walk through the fire . . . the flame will not burn
you. For I the Lord your God, the Holy One of Israel, and
your Savior.*

Isaiah 43:2-3 Holman CSB

As life-here-on-earth unfolds, all of us encounter occasional setbacks: When tough times arrive, we may be forced to rearrange our plans and our priorities. But even on our darkest days, we must remember that God's love remains constant.

The fact that we encounter adversity is not nearly so important as the way we choose to deal with it. When tough times arrive, we have a clear choice: we can begin the difficult work of tackling our troubles . . . or not.

When you summon the courage to face adversity head-on, God will give you the strength to meet any challenge and conquer any hardship. With God as your partner, you can move through—and beyond—any setback. No exceptions.

The closer we are to God, the more confidence we place in him when we are under fire.

C. H. Spurgeon

—Your Thoughts for Today—

_____

_____

_____

_____

OUR WEAKNESS, HIS STRENGTH

The name of the Lord is a strong tower; the righteous run to it and are protected.

Proverbs 18:10 Holman CSB

The line from the children's song is reassuring and familiar: "Little ones to Him belong. We are weak but He is strong." That message applies to kids of all ages: we are all indeed weak, but we worship a mighty God who meets our needs and answers our prayers.

When we sincerely call upon Him, God is a never-ending source of strength and courage. When we are weary, He gives us strength. When we see no hope, God reminds us of His promises. When we grieve, God wipes away our tears. Whatever our circumstances, God will protect us and care for us...if we let Him.

Are you in the midst of adversity or in the grips of temptation? If so, turn to God for strength. The Bible promises that you can do all things through the power of our risen Savior, Jesus Christ. Your challenge, then, is clear: you must place Christ where He belongs: at the very center of your life. When you do, you will discover that, yes, Jesus loves you and that, yes, He will give you direction and strength if you ask it in His name.

—Your Thoughts for Today—

A PRESCRIPTION FOR PANIC

Anxiety in the heart of man causes depression, but a good word makes it glad.

Proverbs 12:25 NKJV

As you make the journey through and beyond cancer, you may be gripped by feelings of anxiety or panic. At times, your anxieties may stem from physical causes—chemical imbalances that cause emotional distress. In such cases, modern medicine offers hope to those who suffer. But oftentimes, our anxieties result from spiritual deficits, not physical ones. And when we're spiritually depleted, the best prescription is found not in the medicine cabinet but deep inside the human heart. What we need is a higher daily dose of God's love, God's peace, God's assurance, and God's presence. And how do we acquire these blessings from our Creator? Through prayer, through meditation, through worship, and through trust.

The thing that preserves a man from panic is his relationship to God.

Oswald Chambers

—Your Thoughts for Today—

_____

_____

_____

_____

_____

NOURISHED BY THE WORD

You will be a good servant of Christ Jesus, nourished by the words of the faith and of the good teaching that you have followed.

1 Timothy 4:6 Holman CSB

As you establish priorities for your journey through and beyond your illness, you must decide whether God's Word will be a bright spotlight that guides your path every day or a tiny nightlight that occasionally flickers in the dark. The decision to study the Bible—or not—is yours and yours alone. But make no mistake: how you choose to use your Bible will have a profound impact on you and your loved ones.

The Bible is the ultimate guide for life; make it your guidebook as well. When you do, you can be comforted in the knowledge that your steps are guided by a Source of wisdom and truth that never fails.

We should approach the Bible with the assurance that here we have God-breathed literature, that it is our privilege and joy to find out what He has to say.

Billy Graham

—Your Thoughts for Today—

_____

_____

_____

_____

_____

A RELATIONSHIP THAT HONORS GOD

My mouth is full of praise and honor to You all day long.
Psalm 71:8 Holman CSB

As you think about the nature of your relationship with God, remember this: you will always have some type of relationship with Him—it is inevitable that your life must be lived in relationship to God. The question is not if you will have a relationship with Him; the burning question is whether or not that relationship will be one that seeks to honor Him.

Are you willing to place God first in your life? And, are you willing to welcome God's Son into your heart? Unless you can honestly answer these questions with a resounding yes, then your relationship with God isn't what it could be or should be. Thankfully, God is always available, He's always ready to forgive, and He's waiting to hear from you now. The rest, of course, is up to you.

Faith is not a feeling; it is action. It is a willed choice.

Elisabeth Elliot

—Your Thoughts for Today—

_____

_____

_____

_____

_____

_____

BUILDING HIS CHURCH

For we are God's fellow workers; you are God's field, you are God's building.

1 Corinthians 3:9 NKJV

The church belongs to God; it is His just as certainly as we are His. When we help build God's church, we bear witness to the changes that He has made in our lives.

Today and every day, let us worship God with grateful hearts and helping hands as we support the church that He has created. Let us witness to our friends, to our families, and to the world. When we do so, we bless others—and we are blessed by the One who sent His Son to die so that we might have eternal life.

Only participation in the full life of a local church builds spiritual muscle.

Rick Warren

—Your Thoughts for Today—

_____

_____

_____

_____

_____

_____

_____

_____

PRIORITIES . . .
MOMENT BY MOMENT

You can't go wrong when you love others. When you add up everything in the law code, the sum total is love. But make sure that you don't get so absorbed and exhausted in taking care of all your day-by-day obligations that you lose track of the time and doze off, oblivious to God.

Romans 13:10-11 MSG

Each waking moment holds the potential to think a creative thought or offer a heartfelt prayer. So even if you're a person with too many demands and not enough energy, don't panic. Instead, be comforted in the knowledge that when you sincerely seek to discover God's priorities for your life, He will provide answers in marvelous and surprising ways.

Remember: this is the day that God has made and that He has filled it with countless opportunities to love, to serve, and to seek His guidance. Seize those opportunities. And as a gift to yourself, to your family, and to the world, slow down and claim the inner peace that is your spiritual birthright: the peace of Jesus Christ. It is yours for the asking. So ask . . . and be thankful.

We are not called to be burden-bearers, but cross-bearers and light-bearers. We must cast our burdens on the Lord.

Corrie ten Boom

—Your Thoughts for Today—

_____

_____

_____

MOUNTAINTOPS AND VALLEYS

I sought the Lord, and He answered me and delivered me from all my fears.

Psalm 34:4 Holman CSB

Every life (including yours) is an unfolding series of events: some fabulous, some not-so-fabulous, and some downright disheartening. When you reach the mountaintops of life, praising God is easy. But, when the storm clouds form overhead, your faith will be tested, sometimes to the breaking point. As a believer, you can take comfort in this fact: Wherever you find yourself, whether at the top of the mountain or the depths of the valley, God is there, and because He cares for you, you can live courageously.

The next time you find your courage tested to the limit, remember that God is your shield and your strength; He is your protector and your deliverer. Call upon Him in your hour of need and He will protect you.

Faith is stronger than fear.

John Maxwell

—Your Thoughts for Today—

_____

_____

_____

_____

_____

_____

ACTIONS THAT REFLECT OUR BELIEFS

If the way you live isn't consistent with what you believe, then it's wrong.

Romans 14:23 MSG

As Christians, we must do our best to ensure that our actions are accurate reflections of our beliefs. Our theology must be demonstrated, not only by our words but, more importantly, by our actions. In short, we should be practical believers, quick to act whenever we see an opportunity to serve God.

Are you the kind of practical Christian who is willing to dig in and do what needs to be done in good times or in tough times? If so, congratulations: God acknowledges your service and blesses it. But if you find yourself more interested in the fine points of theology than in the needs of your neighbors, it's time to rearrange your priorities. God needs believers who are willing to roll up their sleeves and go to work for Him. Count yourself among that number. Theology is a good thing unless it interferes with God's work. And it's up to you to make certain that your theology doesn't.

Do noble things, do not dream them all day long.

Charles Kingsley

—Your Thoughts for Today—

_____

_____

_____

BEYOND ENVY

Therefore, laying aside all malice, all deceit, hypocrisy, envy, and all evil speaking, as newborn babes, desire the pure milk of the word, that you may grow thereby.

1 Peter 2:1-2 NKJV

As we face our own struggles and hardships, we may become envious of those who are spared the burdens we must bear. But God's Word warns us that envy is sin.

As believers, we have absolutely no reason to be envious of any people on earth. After all, as Christians we are already recipients of the greatest gift in all creation: God's grace. We have been promised the gift of eternal life through God's only begotten Son, and we must count that gift as our most precious possession.

So here's a simple suggestion that is guaranteed to bring you happiness: fill your heart with God's love, God's promises, and God's Son . . . and when you do so, leave no room for envy, bitterness, or regret.

———

Discontent dries up the soul.

Elisabeth Elliot

—Your Thoughts for Today—

ENERGIZED FOR LIFE

Be energetic in your life of salvation, reverent and sensitive before God. That energy is God's energy, an energy deep within you, God himself willing and working at what will give him the most pleasure.

Philippians 2:12-13 MSG

The journey through any significant illness is always difficult. So if you're feeling tired, or troubled, or both, don't despair. Your exhaustion is to be expected.

Thankfully, there's always a place you can go to recharge your spiritual batteries. You can turn to God, and He will give you strength. So today and every day, seek strength from the source that never fails. Turn everything over to your Heavenly Father. And rest assured—when you sincerely petition Him, He will give you all the strength you need to live victoriously for Him.

Where there is much prayer, there will be much of the Spirit; where there is much of the Spirit, there will be ever-increasing power.

Andrew Murray

—Your Thoughts for Today—

GOD'S GIFT OF FAMILY

*Choose for yourselves today the one you will worship . . . .
As for me and my family, we will worship the Lord.*

Joshua 24:15 Holman CSB

In the life of every family, there are moments of frustration and disappointment. Lots of them. But, for those who are lucky enough to live in the presence of a close-knit, caring clan, the rewards far outweigh the frustrations. And when times are tough, a loving family is a precious blessing indeed.

No family is perfect, and neither is yours. But, despite the inevitable challenges and hurt feelings of family life, your clan is God's gift to you. That little band of men, women, kids, and babies is a priceless treasure on temporary loan from the Father above. Give thanks to the Giver for the gift of family…and act accordingly.

The only true source of meaning in life is found in love for God and his son Jesus Christ, and love for mankind, beginning with our own families.

James Dobson

—Your Thoughts for Today—

_____

_____

_____

_____

_____

_____

SILENT MOMENTS

Be silent before the Lord and wait expectantly for Him.
Psalm 37:7 Holman CSB

As you struggle to regain your footing after any significant illness, you may become so wrapped up in your daily obligations that you fail to spend quiet time with God. And that's a big mistake.

When you are suffering, you desperately need God. So you should carve out quiet time each day to experience the Father's peace and His love. When you do, God will touch your heart, He will restore your spirits, and He will give you perspective. If you really want to know your Heavenly Father—and if you want to partake in His peace—silence is a wonderful place to start.

It is in that stillness that the Voice will be heard, the only voice in all the universe that speaks peace to the deepest part of us.

Elisabeth Elliot

—Your Thoughts for Today—

THE JOYS OF FRIENDSHIP

I give thanks to my God for every remembrance of you.
Philippians 1:3 Holman CSB

What is a friend? The dictionary defines the word friend as "a person who is attached to another by feelings of affection or personal regard." This definition is accurate, as far as it goes, but when we examine the deeper meaning of friendship, so many more descriptors come to mind: trustworthiness, loyalty, helpfulness, kindness, encouragement, humor, and cheerfulness, to mention but a few.

Today, as you move beyond your illness, and as you consider the many blessings that God has given you, remember to thank Him for the friends He has chosen to place along your path. May you be a blessing to them, and may they richly bless you today, tomorrow, and every day that you live.

───·•◦◦•·───

God has a plan for your friendships because He knows your friends determine the quality and direction of your life.

Charles Stanley

—Your Thoughts for Today—

_____

_____

_____

_____

_____

HIS GENEROSITY . . .
AND YOURS

*But God proves His own love for us in that while we were
still sinners Christ died for us!*

Romans 5:8 Holman CSB

Christ showed His love for us by willingly sacrificing His own life so that we might have eternal
life. We, as Christ's followers, are challenged to
share His love. And, when we walk each day with Jesus—and obey the commandments found in God's Holy
Word—we are worthy ambassadors for Him.

Just as Christ has been—and will always be—the ultimate friend to His flock, so should we be Christlike in
our love and generosity to family members, friends, and
fellow patients. When we share the love of Christ, we
share a priceless gift. As His servants, we must do no less.

The mind grows by taking in, but the heart grows by
giving out.

Warren Wiersbe

—Your Thoughts for Today—

A SERIES OF CHOICES

But seek first the kingdom of God and His righteousness, and all these things will be provided for you.

Matthew 6:33 Holman CSB

Your life is a series of choices. From the instant you wake up in the morning until the moment you nod off to sleep at night, you make countless decisions—decisions about the things you do, decisions about the words you speak, and decisions about the way that you choose to direct your thoughts.

As a believer who has been transformed by the love of Jesus, you have every reason to make wise choices. But sometimes, when the daily grind threatens to grind you up and spit you out, you'll be tempted to say the wrong thing, or do the wrong thing, or both. So, as you pause to consider the kind of Christian you are—and the kind of Christian you want to become—ask yourself whether you're sitting on the fence or standing in the light. The choice is yours . . . and so are the consequences.

———

Every time you make a choice, you are turning the central part of you, the part that chooses, into something a little different from what it was before.

C. S. Lewis

—Your Thoughts for Today—

_____

_____

_____

_____

GOD IS LOVE

He who does not love does not know God, for God is love.
1 John 4:8 NKJV

God loves you. He loves you more than you can imagine; His affection is deeper than you can fathom. God made you in His own image and gave you salvation through the person of His Son Jesus Christ. And as a result, you have an important decision to make. You must decide what to do about God's love: you can return it . . . or not.

When you accept the love that flows from the heart of God, you are transformed. When you embrace God's love, you feel differently about yourself, your neighbors, your community, your church, and your world. When you open your heart to God's love, you will feel compelled to share God's message—and His compassion—with others. God's heart is overflowing—accept His love; return His love; and share His love. Today.

The life of faith is a daily exploration of the constant and countless ways in which God's grace and love are experienced.

Eugene Peterson

—Your Thoughts for Today—

_____

_____

_____

_____

_____

THOUGHTS MATTER

Finally brothers, whatever is true, whatever is honorable, whatever is just, whatever is pure, whatever is lovely, whatever is commendable—if there is any moral excellence and if there is any praise—dwell on these things.

Philippians 4:8 Holman CSB

How will you direct your thoughts today? Will you obey the words of Philippians 4:8 by dwelling upon those things that are honorable, just, and commendable? Or will you allow your thoughts to be hijacked by the negativity that seems to dominate our troubled world? Are you fearful, angry, bored, or worried? Are you so preoccupied with the concerns of this day that you fail to thank God for the promise of eternity? Are you confused, bitter, or pessimistic? If so, God wants to have a little talk with you.

God intends that you experience joy and abundance. So, today and every day hereafter, celebrate the life that God has given you by focusing your thoughts upon those things that are worthy of praise. Today, count your blessings instead of your hardships. And thank the Giver of all things good for gifts that are simply too numerous to count.

—Your Thoughts for Today—

_____

_____

_____

_____

FOR ALL ETERNITY

I assure you: Anyone who hears My word and believes Him who sent Me has eternal life and will not come under judgment, but has passed from death to life.

John 5:24 Holman CSB

Our vision of the future, like our lives here on earth, is limited. God's vision is not burdened by such limitations: His plans extend throughout all eternity. Thus, God's plans for you are not limited to the ups and downs of everyday life. Your Heavenly Father has bigger things in mind . . . much bigger things.

Let us praise the Creator for His priceless gift, and let us share the Good News with all who cross our paths. We return our Father's love by accepting His grace and by sharing His message and His love. When we do, we are blessed here on earth and throughout all eternity.

———

Salvation is God's sudden, calming presence during the stormy seas of our lives.

Max Lucado

—Your Thoughts for Today—

_____

_____

_____

_____

_____

_____

_____

HIS LIMITLESS POWER

The Lord is my light and my salvation; whom shall I fear?
The Lord is the strength of my life; of whom shall I be afraid?

Psalm 27:1 NKJV

Because God's power is limitless, it is far beyond the comprehension of mortal minds. But even though we cannot fully understand the awesome heart of God, we can praise it, worship it, and marvel at its mercy.

When we worship God with faith and assurance, and when we place Him at the absolute center of our lives, we invite His love into our hearts. In turn, we grow to love Him more deeply as we sense His love for us. Today, let us turn our hearts to the Creator, knowing with certainty that His awesome heart has ample room for each of us, and that we, in turn, must make room in our hearts for Him.

If we believe in Jesus Christ, we can face every problem that the world holds.

Oswald Chambers

—Your Thoughts for Today—

_____

_____

_____

_____

_____

_____

THE FUTILITY OF BLAMING OTHERS

Walking down the street, Jesus saw a man blind from birth. His disciples asked, "Rabbi, who sinned: this man or his parents, causing him to be born blind?" Jesus said, "You're asking the wrong question. You're looking for someone to blame. There is no such cause-effect here. Look instead for what God can do."

John 9:1-3 MSG

The blame game seems to be a favorite human pastime. When things go badly, most of us look around for somebody to blame. Yet the blame game is almost never won by those who play it.

Today, instead of looking for someone to blame, look for something to fix, and then get busy fixing it. Instead of directing your anger at people, direct your energy at solving a problem. Focus on your blessings and turn away from bitterness. And as you consider your own situation, remember this: God has a way of helping those who help themselves, but He doesn't spend much time helping those who don't.

Bitterness is the price we charge ourselves for being unwilling to forgive.

Marie T. Freeman

—Your Thoughts for Today—

IN THE FOOTSTEPS OF JESUS

The one who loves his life will lose it, and the one who hates his life in this world will keep it for eternal life. If anyone serves Me, he must follow Me. Where I am, there My servant also will be. If anyone serves Me, the Father will honor him.

John 12:25-26 Holman CSB

As you move through and beyond your illness, you must walk with Jesus every day. Jesus loved you so much that He endured unspeakable humiliation and suffering for you. How will you respond to Christ's sacrifice? Will you take up His cross and follow Him—during good times and hard times—or will you choose another path? When you place your hopes squarely at the foot of the cross, when you place Jesus squarely at the center of your life, you will be transformed.

Do you seek to fulfill God's purpose for your life? Do you seek spiritual abundance? Would you like to partake in "the peace that passes all understanding"? Then follow Christ. Follow Him by picking up His cross today, tomorrow, and every day of your life. When you do, you will quickly discover that Christ's love has the power to change everything, including you.

—Your Thoughts for Today—

FORGIVING AND FORGETTING

But the wisdom from above is first pure, then peace-loving, gentle, compliant, full of mercy and good fruits, without favoritism and hypocrisy.

James 3:17 Holman CSB

D o you have a tough time forgiving and forgetting? If so, welcome to the club. Most of us find it difficult to forgive the people who have hurt us. And that's too bad because life would be much simpler if we could forgive people "once and for all" and be done with it. Yet forgiveness is seldom that easy. Usually, the decision to forgive is straightforward, but the process of forgiving is more difficult. Forgiveness is a journey that requires time, perseverance, and prayer.

If you sincerely wish to forgive someone, pray for that person. And then pray for yourself by asking God to heal your heart. Don't expect forgiveness to be easy or quick, but rest assured: with God as your partner, you can forgive . . . and you will.

———

By not forgiving, by not letting wrongs go, we aren't getting back at anyone. We are merely punishing ourselves by barricading our own hearts.

Jim Cymbala

—Your Thoughts for Today—

_____

_____

_____

_____

A TERRIFIC TOMORROW

"For I know the plans I have for you"—[this is] the Lord's declaration—"plans for [your] welfare, not for disaster, to give you a future and a hope."

Jeremiah 29:11 Holman CSB

How bright do you believe your future to be? Well, if you're a faithful believer, God has plans for you that are intensely and eternally bright.

The way that you think about your treatment and your future will have an important impact on your journey through and beyond your illness. So today, as you live in the present and look to the future, remember that God has an amazing plan for you. Act—and believe—accordingly.

Do not limit the limitless God! With Him, face the future unafraid because you are never alone.

Mrs. Charles E. Cowman

—Your Thoughts for Today—

THE HOPE OF THE WORLD

For the Son of Man has come to save the lost.

Matthew 18:11 Holman CSB

As you reflect upon your priorities for life, the first question you should ask yourself is whether you believe that this life is the only life you'll ever have. If you believe that life here on earth is a one-way ticket to the grave with no hope of an afterlife, then you will most certainly want to plan your affairs accordingly. But, if you believe that God really does sit in His heaven, and if you believe that His Son really did die for your sins, then your priorities for this life must include preparations for the next one.

The hymn by Fanny Crosby contains a familiar refrain: "Tell me the story of Jesus." That story, of course, is one that we cannot tell or hear too often. Jesus is the sovereign friend and ultimate Savior of mankind. Christ showed enduring love for His believers by willingly sacrificing His own life so that we might have eternal life. Now, it is our turn to return His love by inviting Him into our hearts—for Christians, that's priority number 1.

—Your Thoughts for Today—

TRANSCENDENT LOVE

*Who can separate us from the love of Christ? Can affliction
or anguish or persecution or famine or nakedness or danger
or sword? . . . No, in all these things we are more than
victorious through Him who loved us.*

Romans 8:35,37 Holman CSB

Where can we find God's love? Everywhere.
God's love transcends space and time. It
reaches beyond the heavens, and it touch-
es the darkest, smallest corner of every human heart.
When we become passionate in our devotion to the
Father, when we sincerely open our minds and hearts
to Him, His love does not arrive "some day"—it arrives
immediately.

Today, take God at His word and welcome His Son
into your heart. When you do, God's transcendent love
will surround you and transform you, now and forever.

The grace of God transcends all our feeble efforts
to describe it. It cannot be poured into any mental
receptacle without running over.

Vance Havner

—Your Thoughts for Today—

NEW BEGINNINGS

Do not remember the former things, nor consider the things of old. Behold, I will do a new thing.

Isaiah 43:18-19 NKJV

Each new day offers countless opportunities to serve God, to seek His will, and to obey His teachings. But each day also offers countless opportunities to stray from God's commandments and to wander far from His path.

Sometimes, we wander aimlessly in a wilderness of our own making, but God has better plans for us. And, whenever we ask Him to renew our strength and guide our steps, He does so.

Consider this day a new beginning. Consider it a fresh start, a renewed opportunity to serve your Creator with willing hands and a loving heart. Ask God to renew your sense of purpose as He guides your steps. Today is a glorious opportunity to serve your Father in heaven. Seize that opportunity while you can; tomorrow may indeed be too late.

No matter how badly we have failed, we can always get up and begin again. Our God is the God of new beginnings.

Warren Wiersbe

—Your Thoughts for Today—

_____

_____

_____

WHEN PEOPLE ARE DIFFICULT

Then Peter came to Him and said, "Lord, how many times could my brother sin against me and I forgive him? As many as seven times?" "I tell you, not as many as seven," Jesus said to him, "but 70 times seven."

Matthew 18:21-22 Holman CSB

As you move through and beyond your illness, you'll meet new people along the way: doctors, nurses, administrative staff, and fellow patients, to name but a few. Most of these folks will be encouraging and kind, but a few of them may be overly stressed and decidedly unfriendly. So what's a Christian to do? God's answer is straightforward: forgive, forget, and move on. In Luke 6:37, Jesus instructs, "Do not judge, and you will not be judged. Do not condemn, and you will not be condemned. Forgive, and you will be forgiven" (Holman CSB).

Today and every day, make sure that you're quick to forgive others for their shortcomings. And when other people behave badly (as they most certainly will from time to time), don't pay too much attention. Just forgive those people as quickly as you can, and try to move on . . . as quickly as you can.

—Your Thoughts for Today—

TAKING TIME TO ASK

He granted their request because they trusted in Him.

1 Chronicles 5:20 Holman CSB

Sometimes, amid the demands and the frustrations of life-here-on-earth, we forget to slow ourselves down long enough to talk with God. Instead of turning our thoughts and prayers to Him, we rely upon our own resources. Instead of praying for strength and courage, we seek to manufacture it within ourselves. Instead of asking God for guidance, we depend only upon our own limited wisdom. The results of such behaviors are unfortunate and, on occasion, tragic.

Are you in need? Ask God to sustain you. Are you troubled? Take your worries to Him in prayer. Are you weary? Seek God's strength. In all things great and small, in every circumstance, seek God's wisdom and His grace. He hears your prayers, and He will answer. All you must do is ask.

The impossible is exactly what God does.

Oswald Chambers

—Your Thoughts for Today—

THE GUIDEBOOK

All Scripture is inspired by God and is profitable for teaching, for rebuking, for correcting, for training in righteousness, so that the man of God may be complete, equipped for every good work.

2 Timothy 3:16-17 Holman CSB

God has given us a guidebook for righteous living called the Holy Bible. It contains thorough instructions which, if followed, lead to fulfillment, righteousness, and salvation. But, if we choose to ignore God's commandments, the results are as predictable as they are tragic.

God has given us the Bible for the purpose of knowing His promises, His power, His commandments, His wisdom, His love, and His Son. As we study God's teachings and apply them to our lives, we live by the Word that shall never pass away.

The Bible is a Christian's guidebook, and I believe the knowledge it sheds on pain and suffering is the great antidote to fear for suffering people. Knowledge can dissolve fear as light destroys darkness.

Philip Yancey

—Your Thoughts for Today—

_____

_____

_____

_____

_____

LIVING IN CHRIST'S LOVE

So now, little children, remain in Him, so that when He appears we may have boldness and not be ashamed before Him at His coming.

Even though we are imperfect, fallible human beings, even though we have fallen far short of God's commandments, Christ loves us still. His love is perfect and steadfast; it does not waver—it does not change. Our task, as believers, is to accept Christ's love and to encourage others to do likewise.

On the journey through cancer and beyond, you need the love and the peace that is found through the Son of God. Thankfully, Christ's love has no limits; it can encircle all of us. And it's up to each of us to ensure that it does.

If we make our troubles an opportunity to learn more of God's love and His power to aid and bless, then they will teach us to have a firmer confidence in His Providence.

Billy Graham

—Your Thoughts for Today—

OUR ROCK IN
TURBULENT TIMES

And he said: "The Lord is my rock and my fortress and my deliverer; the God of my strength, in whom I will trust."
                                                    2 Samuel 22:2-3 NKJV

Psalm 145 promises, "The Lord is near to all who call on him, to all who call on him in truth. He fulfills the desires of those who fear him; he hears their cry and saves them" (vv. 18-20 NIV). And the words of Jesus offer us comfort: "These things I have spoken to you, that in Me you may have peace. In the world you will have tribulation; but be of good cheer, I have overcome the world" (John 16:33 NKJV).

As believers, we know that God loves us and that He will protect us. In times of hardship, He will comfort us; in times of sorrow, He will dry our tears. When we are troubled, or weak, or sorrowful, God is always with us. We must build our lives on the rock that cannot be shaken: we must trust in God.

The Rock of Ages is the great sheltering encirclement.
                                                    Oswald Chambers

—Your Thoughts for Today—

_____

_____

_____

_____

_____

SAYING YES TO GOD

Fear thou not; for I am with thee.

Isaiah 41:10 KJV

Your decision to seek a deeper relationship with God will not remove all problems from your life; to the contrary, it will bring about a series of personal crises as you constantly seek to say "yes" to God although the world encourages you to do otherwise. Each time you are tempted to distance yourself from the Creator, you will face a spiritual crisis. A few of these crises may be monumental in scope, but most will be the small, everyday decisions of life. In fact, life here on earth can be seen as one test after another—and with each crisis comes yet another opportunity to grow closer to God . . . or to distance yourself from His plan for your life.

Today, you will face many opportunities to say "yes" to your Creator—and you will also encounter many opportunities to say "no" to Him. Your answers will determine the quality of your day and the direction of your life, so answer carefully . . . very carefully.

The Christian life is not a playground; it is a battleground.

Warren Wiersbe

—Your Thoughts for Today—

_____

_____

_____

_____

_____

COMFORTING OTHERS

Carry one another's burdens; in this way you will fulfill the law of Christ.

Galatians 6:2 Holman CSB

We live in a world that is, on occasion, a frightening place. Sometimes, we sustain life-altering losses that are so profound and so tragic that it seems we could never recover. But, with God's help and with the help of encouraging family members and friends, we can recover.

In times of need, God's Word is clear: as believers, we must offer comfort to those in need by sharing not only our courage but also our faith. As the renowned revivalist Vance Havner observed, "No journey is complete that does not lead through some dark valleys. We can properly comfort others only with the comfort wherewith we ourselves have been comforted of God." Enough said.

When action-oriented compassion is absent, it's a telltale sign that something's spiritually amiss.

Bill Hybels

—Your Thoughts for Today—

_____

_____

_____

_____

_____

GOD'S MESSAGE

Listen in silence before me....

Isaiah 41:1 NLT

Billy Graham correctly observed, "Most of us follow our conscience as we follow a wheelbarrow. We push it in front of us in the direction we want to go." To do so, of course, is a profound mistake. Yet all of us, on occasion, have failed to listen to the voice that God planted in our hearts, and all of us have suffered the consequences.

God gave you a conscience for a very good reason: to make your path conform to His will. Wise believers make it a practice to listen carefully to that quiet internal voice. Count yourself among that number. When your conscience speaks, listen and learn. In all likelihood, God is trying to get His message through. And in all likelihood, it is a message that you desperately need to hear.

One of the ways God has revealed Himself to us is in the conscience. Conscience is God's lamp within the human breast.

Billy Graham

—Your Thoughts for Today—

_____

_____

_____

_____

_____

A FRESH OPPORTUNITY

When we were baptized, we were buried with Christ and shared his death. So, just as Christ was raised from the dead by the wonderful power of the Father, we also can live a new life.

Romans 6:4 NCV

God's Word is clear: When we genuinely invite Him to reign over our hearts, and when we accept His transforming love, we are forever changed. When we welcome Christ into our hearts, an old life ends and a new way of living—along with a completely new way of viewing the world—begins.

Each morning offers a fresh opportunity to invite Christ, yet once again, to rule over our hearts and our days. Each morning presents yet another opportunity to take up His cross and follow in His footsteps. Today, let us rejoice in the new life that is ours through Christ, and let us follow Him, step by step, on the path that He first walked.

Shake the dust from your past, and move forward in His promises.

Kay Arthur

—Your Thoughts for Today—

_____

_____

_____

_____

_____

HE REIGNS

In all your ways acknowledge Him, and He shall direct your paths.

Proverbs 3:6 NKJV

G od is sovereign. He reigns over the entire universe and He reigns over your little corner of that universe. Your challenge is to recognize God's sovereignty and live in accordance with His commandments. Sometimes, of course, this is easier said than done.

Your Heavenly Father may not always reveal Himself as quickly (or as clearly) as you would like. But rest assured: God is in control, God is here, and God intends to use you in wonderful, unexpected ways. He desires to lead you along a path of His choosing. Your challenge is to watch, to listen, to learn . . . and to follow.

⸺⸽⸻

We do not understand the intricate pattern of the stars in their course, but we know that He who created them does, and that just as surely as He guides them, He is charting a safe course for us.

Billy Graham

—Your Thoughts for Today—

_____

_____

_____

_____

_____

STANDING ON THE PROMISES

Every word of God is pure; He is a shield to those who put their trust in Him.

Proverbs 30:5 NKJV

A re you standing on the promises of God? Are you expecting God to do wonderful things, or are you living beneath a cloud of apprehension and doubt? The familiar words of Psalm 118:24 remind us of a profound yet simple truth: "This is the day which the LORD hath made; we will rejoice and be glad in it" (KJV). Do you trust that promise, and do you live accordingly? If so, you are living the passionate life that God intends.

For passionate believers, every day begins and ends with God's Son and God's promises. When we accept Christ into our hearts, God promises us the opportunity for earthly peace and spiritual abundance. But more importantly, God promises us the priceless gift of eternal life. As we face the inevitable challenges of life, we must arm ourselves with the promises of God's Holy Word. When we do, we can expect the best, not only for the day ahead, but also for all eternity.

Weave the fabric of God's word through your heart and mind. It will hold strong, even if the rest of life unravels.

Gigi Graham Tchividjian

—Your Thoughts for Today—

_____

_____

_____

HE IS TRUSTWORTHY

The fear of man is a snare, but the one who trusts in the Lord is protected.

Proverbs 29:25 Holman CSB

Sometimes the future seems bright, and sometimes it does not. Yet even when we cannot see the possibilities of tomorrow, God can. As believers, our challenge is to trust an uncertain future to an all-powerful God.

When we trust God, we should trust Him without reservation. We should steel ourselves against the inevitable disappointments of the day, secure in the knowledge that our Heavenly Father has a plan for the future that only He can see.

Can you place your future into the hands of a loving and all-knowing God? Can you live amid the uncertainties of today, knowing that God has dominion over all your tomorrows? If you can, you are wise and you are blessed. When you trust God with everything you are and everything you have, He will bless you now and forever.

Never be afraid to trust an unknown future to a known God.

Corrie ten Boom

—Your Thoughts for Today—

_____

_____

_____

STRENGTH FOR THE STRUGGLE

So because of Christ, I am pleased in weaknesses, in insults, in catastrophes, in persecutions, and in pressures. For when I am weak, then I am strong.

2 Corinthians 12:10 Holman CSB

Life is a tapestry of good days and difficult days, with good days predominating. But when cancer treatment begins, the difficult days may arrive in bunches.

Sometimes, we are tempted to take our blessings for granted (a temptation that we must resist with all our might). But, during life's difficult days, we discover precisely what we're made of. And more importantly, we discover what our faith is made of.

Has your faith been put to the test yet? If so, then you know that with God's help, you can endure life's darker days. But if you have not yet faced the toughest trials, don't worry. When your faith is put to the test, you can be certain that God is perfectly willing—and always ready—to give you the strength you need to overcome any hardship.

—Your Thoughts for Today—

WHY BAD THINGS?

They won't be afraid of bad news; their hearts are steady because they trust the Lord.

Psalm 112:7 NCV

I f God is good, and if He made the world, why do bad things happen? Part of that question is easy to answer, and part of it isn't. Let's get to the easy part first: Sometimes, bad things happen because people disobey God's commandments and invite sadness and heartache into God's beautiful world. But on other occasions, bad things happen, and it's nobody's fault. So who is to blame? Sometimes, nobody is to blame. Sometimes, things just happen and we simply cannot know why. Thankfully, all our questions will be answered . . . some day. The Bible promises that in heaven we will understand all the reasons behind God's plans. But until then, we must simply trust that God is good, and that, in the end, He will make things right.

───•◦∗◦•───

God is God. He knows what he is doing. When you can't trace his hand, trust his heart.

Max Lucado

—Your Thoughts for Today—

_____

_____

_____

_____

_____

BORN AGAIN

You have been born again—not of perishable seed but of imperishable—through the living and enduring word of God.
1 Peter 1:23 Holman CSB

Why did Christ die on the cross? Christ sacrificed His life so that we might be born again. This gift, freely given from God's only begotten Son, is the priceless possession of everyone who accepts Him as Lord and Savior.

Let us claim Christ's gift today. Let us walk with the Savior, let us love Him, let us praise Him, and let us share His message of salvation with all those who cross our paths.

The comforting words of Ephesians 2:8 make God's promise clear: "For by grace you have been saved through faith, and that not of yourselves; it is the gift of God" (NKJV). Thus, we are saved not because of our good deeds but because of our faith in Christ. May we, who have been given so much, praise our Savior for the gift of salvation, and may we share the joyous news of our Master's limitless love with our families, with our friends, and with the world.

———————

Being born again is God's solution to our need for love and life and light.

Anne Graham Lotz

—Your Thoughts for Today—

_____

_____

_____

NO IS AN ANSWER

He granted their request because they trusted in Him.

1 Chronicles 5:20 Holman CSB

God answers our prayers. What God does not do is this: He does not always answer our prayers as soon as we might like, and He does not always answer our prayers by saying "Yes." God isn't an order-taker, and He's not some sort of cosmic vending machine. Sometimes—even when we want something very badly—our loving Heavenly Father responds to our requests by saying "No," and we must accept His answer, even if we don't understand it.

God answers prayers not only according to our wishes but also according to His master plan. We cannot know that plan, but we can know the Planner . . . and we must trust His wisdom, His righteousness, and His love. Always.

———

Let's never forget that some of God's greatest mercies are His refusals. He says no in order that He may, in some way we cannot imagine, say yes.

Elisabeth Elliot

—Your Thoughts for Today—

_____

_____

_____

_____

_____

THE POWER OF
YOUR THOUGHTS

*Be careful what you think, because your thoughts run your
life.*

Proverbs 4:23 NCV

Our thoughts have the power to shape our lives—
for better or worse. Thoughts have the power
to lift our spirits, to improve our circumstances,
and to strengthen our relationship with the Creator.
But, our thoughts also have the power to cause us great
harm if we focus too intently upon the negative aspects
of our lives or ourselves.

When we allow negative thinking to hijack our
emotions, we do harm to our friends, to our families, and
to ourselves. So we must guard our hearts against negativity, cynicism, and despair.

Today, make your thoughts an offering to God.
Seek—by the things you think and the actions you
take—to honor Him and serve Him. He deserves no
less. And neither, for that matter, do you.

Your thoughts are the determining factor as to whose
mold you are conformed to. Control your thoughts and
you control the direction of your life.

Charles Stanley

—Your Thoughts for Today—

_____

_____

_____

SOLVING PROBLEMS

People who do what is right may have many problems, but the Lord will solve them all.

Psalm 34:19 NCV

L ife is an exercise in problem-solving. The question is not whether we will encounter problems; the real question is how we will choose to address them. The words of Psalm 34 remind us that the Lord solves problems for "people who do what is right." And usually, doing "what is right" means doing the uncomfortable work of confronting our challenges head on.

If you're facing tough medical treatments or the tough times that accompany them, don't give up and don't give in. Just ask God for the strength you need today, and do your best to solve today's problems. When you do, you and your Heavenly Father can accomplish miracles, one day at a time.

We are all faced with a series of great opportunities, brilliantly disguised as unsolvable problems. Unsolvable without God's wisdom, that is.

Charles Swindoll

—Your Thoughts for Today—

_____

_____

_____

_____

_____

CONFIDENT CHRISTIANITY

You are my hope; O Lord GOD, You are my confidence.
Psalm 71:5 NASB

We Christians have many reasons to be confident. God is in His heaven; Christ has risen, and we are the sheep of His flock. Yet sometimes, even the most devout Christians can become discouraged. Discouragement, however, is not God's way; He is a God of possibility not negativity.

Are you a confident Christian? You should be. God's grace is eternal and His promises are unambiguous. So count your blessings, not your hardships. And live courageously. God is the Giver of all things good, and He watches over you today and forever.

———————

Bible hope is confidence in the future.

Warren Wiersbe

—Your Thoughts for Today—

_____

_____

_____

_____

_____

_____

_____

CRITICS BEWARE

Don't pick on people, jump on their failures, criticize their faults—unless, of course, you want the same treatment. Don't condemn those who are down; that hardness can boomerang. Be easy on people; you'll find life a lot easier.

Luke 6:37 MSG

From experience, we know that it is easier to criticize than to correct. And we know that it is easier to find faults than solutions. Yet the urge to criticize others remains a powerful temptation for most of us. Our task, as obedient believers, is to break the twin habits of negative thinking and critical speech.

Negativity is highly contagious: we give it to others who, in turn, give it back to us. This cycle can be broken by positive thoughts, heartfelt prayers, and encouraging words. As thoughtful servants of a loving God, we can use the transforming power of Christ's love to break the chains of negativity. And we should.

The scrutiny we give other people should be for ourselves.

Oswald Chambers

—Your Thoughts for Today—

_____

_____

_____

_____

_____

FIRST THINGS FIRST

Steep your life in God-reality, God-initiative, God-provisions. Don't worry about missing out. You'll find all your everyday human concerns will be met.

Matthew 6:33 MSG

Have you fervently asked God to help prioritize your life and your recovery? Have you asked Him for guidance and for the courage to do the things that you know need to be done? If so, then you're continually inviting your Creator to reveal Himself in a variety of ways.

When you make God a full partner in every aspect of your healing, He will lead you along the proper path: His path. When you allow God to reign over your heart, He will honor you with spiritual blessings that are simply too numerous to count. So, as you plan for the day ahead, make God's will your ultimate priority. When you do, your daily to-do list will take care of itself.

The moment you wake up each morning, all your wishes and hopes for the day rush at you like wild animals. And the first job each morning consists in shoving it all back; in listening to that other voice, taking that other point of view, letting that other, larger, stronger, quieter life coming flowing in.

C. S. Lewis

—Your Thoughts for Today—

_____

_____

_____

DOUBT AND
THE TRUE BELIEVER

Immediately the father of the child cried out and said with tears, "Lord, I believe; help my unbelief!"

Mark 9:24 NKJV

Even the most faithful Christians are overcome by occasional bouts of fear and doubt. You are no different. When you feel that your faith is being tested to its limits, seek the comfort and assurance of the One who sent His Son as a sacrifice for you.

Every life—including yours—is a series of successes and failures, celebrations and disappointments, joys and sorrows, hopes and doubts. But even when you feel very distant from God, God is never distant from you. When you sincerely seek His presence, He will touch your heart, calm your fears, and restore your faith in the future . . . and your faith in Him.

There is a difference between doubt and unbelief. Doubt is a matter of mind: we cannot understand what God is doing or why He is doing it. Unbelief is a matter of will: we refuse to believe God's Word and obey what He tells us to do.

Warren Wiersbe

—Your Thoughts for Today—

_____

_____

_____

_____

SERENITY NOW

Do not remember the past events, pay no attention to things of old. Look, I am about to do something new; even now it is coming. Do you not see it? Indeed, I will make a way in the wilderness, rivers in the desert.

Isaiah 43:18-19 Holman CSB

The American theologian Reinhold Niebuhr composed a profoundly simple verse that came to be known as the Serenity Prayer: "God, grant me the serenity to accept the things I cannot change, the courage to change the things I can, and the wisdom to know the difference." Niebuhr's words are far easier to recite than they are to live by, especially for people who are fighting a serious illness. After all, most of us want life to unfold in accordance with our own wishes and timetables. But sometimes God has other plans.

If you've encountered unfortunate circumstances that seem beyond your power to control, don't give up, don't give in, and don't lose faith. Turn all your concerns over to God, and trust Him to manage the things that you can't. When you do, you can be comforted in the knowledge that your Creator is both loving and wise, and that He understands His plans perfectly, even when you do not.

—Your Thoughts for Today—

_____

_____

_____

_____

TRUST HIS TIMING

He has made everything appropriate in its time. He has also put eternity in their hearts, but man cannot discover the work God has done from beginning to end.

Ecclesiastes 3:11 Holman CSB

The Bible teaches us to trust God's timing in all matters, but we are sorely tempted to do otherwise, especially when our hearts are breaking. We pray (and trust) that we will find peace some day, and we want it NOW. God, however, works on His own timetable, and His schedule does not always coincide with ours.

God's plans are perfect; ours most certainly are not. Thus we must learn to trust the Father in good times and hard times.

Elisabeth Elliot advised, "We must learn to move according to the timetable of the Timeless One, and to be at peace." So today, as you make the journey with God through illness and beyond it, be patient, be faithful, and be brave. God is still in charge, and you are still protected.

———

God knows exactly how much you can take, and He will never permit you to reach a breaking point.

Barbara Johnson

—Your Thoughts for Today—

_____

_____

_____

HAPPINESS AND HOLINESS

Happy are the people who live at your Temple . . . . Happy are those whose strength comes from you.

Psalm 84:4-5 NKJV

When you're battling a serious illness, it may be hard to think happy thoughts. Hard, but not impossible.

Do you seek happiness, abundance, and contentment? If so, here are some things you should do: Love God and His Son; depend upon God for strength; try, to the best of your abilities, to follow God's will; and strive to obey His Holy Word. When you do these things, you'll discover that happiness goes hand-in-hand with righteousness. The happiest people are not those who rebel against God; the happiest people are those who love God and obey His commandments.

Joy is the serious business of heaven.

C. S. Lewis

—Your Thoughts for Today—

_____

_____

_____

_____

_____

_____

PRAY SPECIFICALLY

So I say to you, keep asking, and it will be given to you. Keep searching, and you will find. Keep knocking, and the door will be opened to you.

Luke 11:9 Holman CSB

As the old saying goes, if it's big enough to worry about, it's big enough to pray about. Yet sometimes, we don't pray about the specific details of our lives or our treatment. Instead, we may offer general prayers that are decidedly heavy on platitudes and decidedly light on particulars.

The next time you pray, try this: be very specific about the things you ask God to do. Of course God already knows precisely what you need—He knows infinitely more about your life than you do—but you need the experience of talking to your Creator in honest, unambiguous language.

So today, don't be vague with God. Tell Him exactly what you need. He doesn't need to hear the details, but you do.

When you ask God to do something, don't ask timidly; put your whole heart into it.

Marie T. Freeman

—Your Thoughts for Today—

_____

_____

_____

_____

TERMINATING THE TANTRUM

Don't make friends with an angry man, and don't be a companion of a hot-tempered man, or you will learn his ways and entangle yourself in a snare.

Proverbs 22:24-25 Holman CSB

Anger and cancer are often traveling companions. But, uncontrolled anger can be destructive. Temper tantrums are usually unproductive, unattractive, unforgettable, and unnecessary. Perhaps that's why Proverbs 16:32 states that, "Controlling your temper is better than capturing a city" (NCV).

If you've allowed anger to become a regular visitor at your house, today you must pray for wisdom, for patience, and for a heart that is so filled with love and forgiveness that it contains no room for bitterness. God will help you terminate your tantrums if you ask Him to. And God can help you perfect your ability to be patient if you only ask.

Anger is the noise of the soul; the unseen irritant of the heart; the relentless invader of silence.

Max Lucado

—Your Thoughts for Today—

_____

_____

_____

_____

_____

THE GREATEST OF THESE

And now abide faith, hope, love, these three; but the greatest of these is love.

1 Corinthians 13:13 NKJV

The beautiful words of 1st Corinthians 13 remind us that love is God's commandment: Faith is important, of course. So, too, is hope. But, love is more important still. We are commanded (not advised, not encouraged…commanded!) to love one another just as Christ loved us (John 13:34). That's a tall order, but as Christians, we are obligated to follow it.

Christ showed His love for us on the cross, and we are called upon to return Christ's love by sharing it. Today, let us spread Christ's love to families, friends, and even strangers, so that through us, others might come to know Him.

The best use of life is love. The best expression of love is time. The best time to love is now.

Rick Warren

—Your Thoughts for Today—

A PASSIONATE LIFE

Do not lack diligence; be fervent in spirit; serve the Lord.
Romans 12:11 Holman CSB

Are you passionate about your life, your loved ones, your work, and your faith? As a believer who has been saved by a risen Christ, you should be.

As a thoughtful Christian, you have every reason to be enthusiastic about life. But sometimes, the inevitable struggles of the journey through and beyond your illness may leave you feeling decidedly unenthusiastic. If you feel that your enthusiasm is slowly fading away, it's time to slow down, to rest, to count your blessings, and to pray. When you feel worried or weary, you must pray fervently for God to renew your sense of wonderment and excitement.

Life with God is a glorious adventure; revel in it. When you do, God will most certainly smile upon your work and your life.

This is Christianity as God intended it—a passionate, willful, and fully emotional relationship.

Bill Hybels

—Your Thoughts for Today—

_____

_____

_____

_____

_____

HIS JOY . . . AND YOURS

Rejoice in the Lord always. I will say it again: Rejoice!
Philippians 4:4 Holman CSB

Christ made it clear: He intends that His joy should become our joy. Yet sometimes, amid the inevitable challenges of life-here-on-earth, we can forfeit—albeit temporarily—the joy of Christ as we wrestle with illness, grief, or hardship.

Billy Graham correctly observed, "When Jesus Christ is the source of our joy, no words can describe it." And C. S. Lewis noted that, "Joy is the serious business of heaven." So here's a prescription for better spiritual health: Open the door of your soul to Christ. When you do, He will share His peace and His joy. And you'll be blessed today, tomorrow, and forever.

Christ and joy go together.

E. Stanley Jones

—Your Thoughts for Today—

GIVE ME PATIENCE, LORD, RIGHT NOW!

And we exhort you, brothers: warn those who are lazy, comfort the discouraged, help the weak, be patient with everyone.

1 Thessalonians 5:14 Holman CSB

Most of us are impatient for God to grant us the desires of our heart. Usually, we know what we want, and we know precisely when we want it: right now, if not sooner. And so it is with healing: we naturally want instant recovery, and we want it now. But God may have other plans. And when God's plans differ from our own, we must trust in His infinite wisdom and in His infinite love.

As busy people living in a fast-paced world, many of us find that waiting quietly for God is difficult. But God instructs us to be patient in all things. We must be patient with our families, our friends, and our doctors. We must also be patient with our Creator as He unfolds His plan for our lives. And that's as it should be. After all, think how patient God has been with us.

Be patient. God is using today's difficulties to strengthen you for tomorrow. He is equipping you. The God who makes things grow will help you bear fruit.

Max Lucado

—Your Thoughts for Today—

_____

_____

_____

THE POWER OF WORDS

A word fitly spoken is like apples of gold in settings of silver.
Proverbs 25:11 NKJV

The words we speak are important. Our words have the power to uplift others or to discourage them. And thoughtless words, spoken in haste, cannot be erased.

All too often, in the rush to have ourselves heard, we speak first and think next…with unfortunate results. Yet God's Word reminds us that, "Reckless words pierce like a sword, but the tongue of the wise brings healing" (Proverbs 12:18 NIV).

Today, measure your words carefully. Use words of kindness and praise, not words of anger or derision. Remember that you have the power to heal others, to help others, or to injure them. Your words have the power to lift others up or to hold them back. When you lift them up, your wisdom will bring healing and comfort to a world that needs both.

God grant that we may not hinder those who are battling their way slowly into the light.

Oswald Chambers

—Your Thoughts for Today—

_____

_____

_____

_____

_____

THY WILL BE DONE

Sheathe your sword! Should I not drink the cup that the Father has given Me?

John 18:11 Holman CSB

As we journey through and beyond the struggles of life, all of us must, from time to time, endure days filled with anxiety and pain. And, as human beings with limited understanding, we can never fully understand the plans of our Father in heaven. But as believers in a benevolent God, we must always trust Him.

When Jesus went to the Mount of Olives, He poured out His heart to God (Luke 22). Jesus knew of the agony that He was destined to endure, but He also knew that God's will must be done.

We, like our Savior, face trials that bring fear and trembling to the very depths of our souls, but like Christ, we, too, must seek God's will, not our own. When we learn to accept God's will without reservation, we experience the peace that He offers to wise believers who trust Him completely.

Our Lord never asks us to decide for Him; He asks us to yield to Him—a very different matter.

Oswald Chambers

—Your Thoughts for Today—

INFINITE POSSIBILITIES

But He said, "The things which are impossible with men are possible with God."

Luke 18:27 NKJV

What does life have in store for you? A world full of possibilities (of course it's up to you to seize them) and God's promise of abundance (of course it's up to you to accept it). Your Creator has blessed you beyond measure. Honor Him with your prayers, your words, your deeds, and your joy.

When God is involved, anything can happen.

Charles Swindoll

—Your Thoughts for Today—

MENTORS THAT MATTER

The lips of the righteous feed many.

Proverbs 10:21 Holman CSB

Here's a simple yet effective way to strengthen your faith: Choose role models whose faith in God is strong.

When you emulate godly people, you become a more godly person yourself. That's why you should seek out mentors who, by their words and their presence, make you a better person and a better Christian.

Today, as a gift to yourself, select, from friends, family members, or fellow patients, a mentor whose judgement you trust. Then listen carefully to your mentor's advice and be willing to accept that advice, even if accepting it requires effort, or pain, or both. Consider your mentor to be God's gift to you. Thank God for that gift, and use it for the glory of His kingdom.

God often keeps us on the path by guiding us through the counsel of friends and trusted spiritual advisors.

Bill Hybels

—Your Thoughts for Today—

_____

_____

_____

_____

_____

_____

THE POWER OF FAITH

Believe in the Lord your God, and you will be established; believe in His prophets, and you will succeed.

2 Chronicles 20:20 Holman CSB

Every life—including yours—is a series of celebrations and disappointments, joys and sorrows, successes and failure. Every step of the way, through every triumph and tragedy, God will stand by your side and strengthen you . . . if you have faith in Him. Jesus taught His disciples that if they had faith, they could move mountains. You can too.

When you place your faith, your trust, indeed your life in the hands of Christ Jesus, you'll be amazed at the marvelous things He can do with you and through you. So strengthen your faith through praise, through worship, through Bible study, and through prayer. And trust God's plans. With Him, all things are possible, and He stands ready to open a world of possibilities to you . . . if you have faith.

———

Let your faith in Christ be in the quiet confidence that He will, every day and every moment, give you the strength you need.

Andrew Murray

—Your Thoughts for Today—

_____

_____

_____

_____

MAKING PEACE
WITH YOUR PAST

The Lord says, "Forget what happened before, and do not think about the past. Look at the new thing I am going to do. It is already happening. Don't you see it? I will make a road in the desert and rivers in the dry land."

Isaiah 43:18-19 NCV

Have you made peace with your past? If so, congratulations. But, if you are mired in the quicksand of regret, it's time to plan your escape. How can you do so? By accepting what has been and by trusting God for what will be.

Because you are human, you may be slow to forget yesterday's disappointments. But, if you sincerely seek to focus your hopes and energies on the future, then you must find ways to accept the past, no matter how difficult it may be to do so. So, if you have not yet made peace with the past, today is the day to declare an end to all hostilities. When you do, you can then turn your thoughts to wondrous promises of God and to the glorious future that He has in store for you.

———

Don't let yesterday use up too much of today.

Dennis Swanberg

—Your Thoughts for Today—

_____

_____

_____

_____

THE COURAGE TO PERSEVERE

Should we accept only good from God and not adversity?
                                        Job 2:10 Holman CSB

If you're battling a serious illness, you need perseverance, and lots of it. The reassuring words of Hebrews 10:36 serve as a comforting reminder that perseverance indeed pays: "You have need of endurance, so that when you have done the will of God, you may receive what was promised" (NASB).

Are you willing to trust God's Word? And are you willing to keep "fighting the good fight," even when you've experienced unexpected setbacks? If so, you may soon be surprised at the creative ways that God finds to help determined people like you . . . people who possess the wisdom and the courage to persevere.

The battles of life are not easy, but God has given us the equipment we need to succeed.

                                        Warren Wiersbe

—Your Thoughts for Today—

_____

_____

_____

_____

_____

_____

_____

LOOKING FOR OPPORTUNITIES

Make the most of every opportunity.

Colossians 4:5 NIV

As you journey through and beyond your illness, you'll have many opportunities to serve. It's up to you to seize those opportunities whenever you can.

God's hand shapes the world, and it shapes your life. So wherever you find yourself—whether on the mountaintop or in the darkest valley—remember that God is there, too. And He's ready to help. Are you willing to accept God's help by prayerfully opening your heart to Him? And are you willing to conform your will to His? If so, then you can be certain that you and God, working together, will make the most of whatever comes your way.

Life is a glorious opportunity.

Billy Graham

—Your Thoughts for Today—

THE POWER OF SILENCE

My soul, wait silently for God alone, for my expectation is from Him.

Psalm 62:5 NKJV

The world seems to grow louder day by day, and our senses seem to be invaded at every turn. But, if we allow the distractions of a clamorous society to separate us from God's peace, we do ourselves a profound disservice. Our task, as dutiful believers, is to carve out moments of silence in a world filled with noise.

If we are to maintain righteous minds and compassionate hearts, we must take time each day for prayer and for meditation. We must make ourselves still in the presence of our Creator. We must quiet our minds and our hearts so that we might sense God's will and His love.

———

Recently I've been learning that life comes down to this: God is in everything. Regardless of what difficulties I am experiencing at the moment, or what things aren't as would like them to be, I look at the circumstances and say, "Lord, what are you trying to teach me?"

Catherine Marshall

—Your Thoughts for Today—

_____

_____

_____

_____

LET GOD DECIDE

A man's heart plans his way, but the Lord directs his steps.
Proverbs 16:9 NKJV

Are you facing a difficult decision? If so, it's time to step back, to stop focusing on the world, and to focus, instead, on the will of your Father in heaven. The world will often lead you astray, but God will not. His counsel leads you to Himself, which, of course, is the path He has always intended for you to take.

Everyday living is an exercise in decision-making. Today and every day you must make choices: choices about what you will do, what you will worship, and how you will think. When in doubt, make choices that you sincerely believe will bring you to a closer relationship with God. And if you're uncertain of your next step, pray about it. When you do, answers will come—the right answers for you.

God always gives His best to those who leave the choice with Him.

Jim Elliot

—Your Thoughts for Today—

_____

_____

_____

_____

_____

BEYOND THE DIFFICULTIES

When you are in distress and all these things have happened to you, you will return to the Lord your God in later days and obey Him. He will not leave you, destroy you, or forget the covenant with your fathers that He swore to them by oath, because the Lord your God is a compassionate God.

Deuteronomy 4:30-31 Holman CSB

Sometimes things go wrong . . . very wrong. But, when we find ourselves overtaken by the disappointments of life, we must catch ourselves, take a deep breath, and lift our thoughts upward. Although we are here on earth struggling to rise above the distractions of the day, we need never struggle alone. God is here—eternally and faithfully, with infinite patience and love—and, if we reach out to Him, He will restore perspective and peace to our souls.

If you find yourself enduring difficult circumstances, remember that God remains in His heaven. If you become discouraged with the direction of your day or your life, lift your thoughts and prayers to Him. He will guide you through your difficulties and beyond them.

Whatever hallway you're in—no matter how long, how dark, or how scary—God is right there with you.

Bill Hybels

When life is difficult, God wants us to have a faith that trusts and waits.

Kay Arthur

Grace grows best in the winter.

C. H. Spurgeon

When God allows extraordinary trials for His people, He prepares extraordinary comforts for them.

Corrie ten Boom

The task ahead of us is never as great as the Power behind us.

Anonymous

—Your Thoughts for Today—

PROTECTED

Be of good courage, and He shall strengthen your heart, all you who hope in the Lord.

Psalm 31:24 NKJV

Dealing with a diagnosis of cancer is no easy task. It's a time of uncertainty and fear, a time when even the most courageous Christian has cause for concern. But as believers we can live boldly, knowing that we have been saved by a loving Father and His only begotten Son.

Are you in need? Ask God to sustain you. Are you troubled? Take your worries to Him, and He will comfort you. Are you weary? Seek God's strength. Do you have questions about your future that you simply can't answer? Ask your Heavenly Father for insight and direction. In all things great and small, seek God's wisdom and His will. He will hear your prayers, and He will answer.

Seeing that a Pilot steers the ship in which we sail, who will never allow us to perish even in the midst of shipwrecks, there is no reason why our minds should be overwhelmed with fear and overcome with weariness.

John Calvin

—Your Thoughts for Today—

_____

_____

_____

_____

_____

FAITH VERSUS FEAR

Do not fear, for I am with you; do not be afraid, for I am your God. I will strengthen you; I will help you; I will hold on to you with My righteous right hand.

Isaiah 41:10 Holman CSB

A terrible storm rose quickly on the Sea of Galilee, and the disciples were afraid. Although they had witnessed many miracles, the disciples feared for their lives, so they turned to Jesus, and He calmed the waters and the wind.

The next time you find yourself facing a fear-provoking situation, remember that the One who calmed the wind and the waves is also your personal Savior. Then ask yourself which is stronger: your faith or your fear. The answer should be obvious. So, when the storm clouds form overhead and you find yourself being tossed on the stormy seas of life, remember this: Wherever you are, God is there, too. And, because He cares for you, you are protected.

The Lord Jesus by His Holy Spirit is with me, and the knowledge of His presence dispels the darkness and allays any fears.

Bill Bright

—Your Thoughts for Today—

_____

_____

_____

_____

A PLACE OF WORSHIP

For where two or three are gathered together in My name, I am there among them.

Matthew 18:20 Holman CSB

The Bible teaches that we should worship God in our hearts and in our churches. We have clear instructions to "feed the church of God" and to worship our Creator in the presence of fellow believers.

We live in a world that is teeming with temptations and distractions—a world where good and evil struggle in a constant battle to win our minds, our hearts, and our souls. Our challenge, of course, is to ensure that we cast our lot on the side of God. One way that we remain faithful to Him is through the practice of regular, purposeful worship with our families. When we worship the Father faithfully and fervently, we are blessed.

❧

The New Testament does not envisage solitary religion; some kind of regular assembly for worship and instruction is everywhere taken for granted in the epistles.

C. S. Lewis

—Your Thoughts for Today—

_____

_____

_____

_____

_____

_____

THE CHAINS OF PERFECTIONISM

*Those who wait for perfect weather will never plant seeds;
those who look at every cloud will never harvest crops.*

Ecclesiastes 11:4 NCV

Perhaps your appearance has changed. Or perhaps you're unable to do things that you once took for granted. If so, you may have become just a little too self-critical for your own good.

The media delivers an endless stream of messages that tell you how to look and how to behave. The media's expectations are impossible to meet—God's are not. God doesn't expect perfection . . . and neither should you. After all, pleasing God is simply a matter of obeying His commandments and accepting His Son. But as for pleasing everybody else? That's impossible.

Being loved by Him whose opinion matters most gives us the security to risk loving, too—even loving ourselves.

Gloria Gaither

—Your Thoughts for Today—

THY WILL BE DONE

"Father, if it is Your will, take this cup away from Me; nevertheless not My will, but Yours, be done."

Luke 22:42 NKJV

As human beings with limited understanding, we can never fully comprehend the will of God. But as believers in a benevolent God, we must always trust the will of our Heavenly Father.

Before His crucifixion, Jesus went to the Mount of Olives and poured out His heart to God. Jesus knew of the agony that He was destined to endure, but He also knew that God's will must be done. We, like our Savior, face trials that bring fear and trembling to the very depths of our souls, but like Christ, we, too, must ultimately seek God's will, not our own. When we entrust our lives to Him completely and without reservation, He gives us the strength to meet any challenge, the courage to face any trial, and the wisdom to live in His righteousness.

"If the Lord will" is not just a statement on a believer's lips; it is the constant attitude of his heart.

Warren Wiersbe

—Your Thoughts for Today—

FOCUSING ON HEAVEN

Since you have been raised to new life with Christ, set your sights on the realities of heaven, where Christ sits at God's right hand in the place of honor and power.

Colossians 3:1 NLT

The Bible promises that when you give your heart to Jesus, you will live forever with Him in heaven. It's an incredible promise with powerful implications for you and your illness.

C. S. Lewis advised, "We ought to give thanks for all fortune: if it is 'good,' because it is good, if 'bad' because it works in us patience, humility and the contempt of this world and the hope of our eternal country."

As you endure the challenges of your illness and the demands of your treatment, keep your heart and thoughts focused on eternity. When you do, you'll keep your problems—and God's promises—in proper perspective.

Even life's happiest experiences last but a moment, yet Heaven's joy is eternal.

Billy Graham

—Your Thoughts for Today—

_____

_____

_____

_____

_____

HIS COMFORTING HAND

But God, who comforts the humble, comforted us . . . .
2 Corinthians 7:6 Holman CSB

If you have been touched by the transforming hand of Jesus, then you have every reason to live courageously. Still, even if you are a dedicated Christian, you may find yourself discouraged by the challenges of ill health or the inevitable disappointments that befall us all.

The next time you find your courage tested to the limit, lean upon God's promises. Trust His Son. Remember that God is always near and that He is your protector and your deliverer. When you are worried, anxious, or afraid, call upon Him and accept the touch of His comforting hand. Remember that God rules both mountaintops and valleys—with limitless wisdom and love—now and forever.

———

God's promises are medicine for the broken heart. Let Him comfort you. And, after He has comforted you, try to share that comfort with somebody else. It will do both of you good.

Warren Wiersbe

—Your Thoughts for Today—

GOD NEVER LEAVES YOU

The eyes of the Lord are in every place, keeping watch . . . .
Proverbs 15:3 NKJV

As you make the journey through and beyond your illness, you may become discourage, and you may feel alone. But in truth, you are never alone, not even for a moment. God is always with you, always as near as your next breath, as close as your next thought. So the next time you're feeling unconnected from your family, or from your friends, or from your community, remind yourself of God's presence. God's love is constant; His protection is eternal; His plans are perfect. Trust Him today and every day, beginning now and ending never.

Have courage for the great sorrows of life and patience for the small ones; and when you have laboriously accomplished your daily task, go to sleep in peace. God is awake.

Victor Hugo

—Your Thoughts for Today—

ANGRY?

Patience is better than power, and controlling one's temper, than capturing a city.

Does cancer make you angry? If so, you are certainly not alone. The journey through and beyond cancer may be the toughest challenge you'll ever face. So you have every right to be upset at your circumstances . . . but please don't be upset with God.

God's love for you is greater than you can imagine. And, your Father has promised to protect you today and forever. So, as you take the next step in your life's journey, make God your traveling companion. You need Him; He loves you; and you are protected. So try not to be angry. Try, instead, to be grateful.

———

Get rid of the poison of built-up anger and the acid of long-term resentment.

Charles Swindoll

—Your Thoughts for Today—

_____

_____

_____

_____

_____

_____

_____

THE RIGHT KIND OF ATTITUDE

May the words of my mouth and the meditation of my heart be acceptable to You, Lord, my rock and my Redeemer.
Psalm 19:14 Holman CSB

What is your attitude today? Are you fearful or worried? Are you bitter, confused, cynical or pessimistic? If so, it's time to have a little chat with your Father in heaven.

God intends that your life be filled with spiritual abundance and joy—but God will not force His joy upon you—you must claim it for yourself. So do yourself this favor: accept God's gifts with a smile on your face, a song on your lips, and joy in your heart. Think optimistically about yourself, your health, and your future. Give thanks to the One who has given you everything, and trust in your heart that He wants to give you so much more.

The things we think are the things that feed our souls. If we think on pure and lovely things, we shall grow pure and lovely like them; and the converse is equally true.
Hannah Whitall Smith

—Your Thoughts for Today—

_____

_____

_____

_____

_____

BEHAVIOR REFLECTS BELIEF

As you have therefore received Christ Jesus the Lord, so walk in Him, rooted and built up in Him and established in the faith, as you have been taught, abounding in it with thanksgiving.

Colossians 2:6-7 NKJV

As Christians, we must do our best to make sure that our actions are accurate reflections of our beliefs. Our theology must be demonstrated, not only by our words but, more importantly, by our actions. In short, we should be practical believers, quick to act whenever we see an opportunity to serve God.

English clergyman Thomas Fuller observed, "He does not believe who does not live according to his beliefs." These words are most certainly true. Like it or not, your life is an accurate reflection of your creed. If this fact gives you cause for concern, don't bother talking about the changes that you intend to make—make them. And then, when your good deeds speak for themselves—as they most certainly will—don't interrupt.

Obedience is the natural outcome of belief.

C. H. Spurgeon

—Your Thoughts for Today—

REJOICE ALWAYS

Rejoice in the Lord always. Again I will say, rejoice!

Philippians 4:4 NKJV

Oswald Chambers correctly observed, "Joy is the great note all throughout the Bible." C. S. Lewis echoed that thought when he wrote, "Joy is the serious business of heaven." But, even the most dedicated Christians can, on occasion, forget to celebrate each day for what it is: a priceless gift from God.

Today, celebrate life as God intended. Today, share the Good News of Jesus Christ. Today, no matter your circumstances, put a smile on your face, kind words on your lips, and a song in your heart. And then, when you have celebrated life to the fullest, invite others to do likewise. After all, this is God's day, and He has given us clear instructions for its use. We are commanded to rejoice and be glad. So, with no further ado, let the celebration begin...

God has a course mapped out for your life, and all the inadequacies in the world will not change His mind. He will be with you every step of the way. And though it may take time, He has a celebration planned for when you cross over the "Red Seas" of your life.

Charles Swindoll

—Your Thoughts for Today—

THE GIFT OF CHEERFULNESS

Anxiety in a man's heart weighs it down, but a good word cheers it up.

Proverbs 12:25 Holman CSB

Cheerfulness is a gift that we give to others and to ourselves. And, as believers who have been saved by a risen Christ, why shouldn't we be cheerful? The answer, of course, is that we have every reason to honor our Savior with joy in our hearts, smiles on our faces, and words of celebration on our lips.

Christ promises us lives of abundance and joy if we accept His love and His grace. Yet sometimes, even the most righteous among us are beset by fits of ill temper, sadness, and frustration. During these moments, we may not feel like turning our thoughts and prayers to Christ, but that's precisely what we should do. When we do so, we simply can't stay grumpy for long.

The people whom I have seen succeed best in life have always been cheerful and hopeful people who went about their business with a smile on their faces.

Charles Kingsley

—Your Thoughts for Today—

OBEDIENCE NOW

This is how we are sure that we have come to know Him: by keeping His commands.

1 John 2:3 Holman CSB

In order to enjoy a deeper relationship with God, you must strive diligently to live in accordance with His commandments. But there's a problem—you live in a world that seeks to snare your attention and lead you away from God.

Because you are an imperfect mortal being, you cannot be perfectly obedient, nor does God expect you to be. What is required, however, is a sincere desire to be obedient coupled with an awareness of sin and a willingness to distance yourself from it as soon as you encounter it.

Are you willing to conform your behavior to God's rules? Hopefully, you can answer that question with a resounding yes. Otherwise, you'll never experience a full measure of the blessings that the Creator gives to those who obey Him.

———

We grow spiritually as our Lord grew physically: by a life of simple, unobtrusive obedience.

Oswald Chambers

—Your Thoughts for Today—

_____

_____

_____

_____

THE SOURCE OF ALL COMFORT

When doubts filled my mind, your comfort gave me renewed hope and cheer.

Psalm 94:19 NLT

In times of adversity, we are wise to remember the words of Jesus, who, when He walked on the waters, reassured His disciples, saying, "Take courage! It is I. Don't be afraid" (Matthew 14:27 NIV). Then, with Christ on His throne—and with trusted friends and loving family members at our sides—we can face our fears with courage and with faith.

Are you facing a difficult challenge or a serious setback? If so, remember that no problem is too big for God . . . not even yours.

———

How changed our lives would be if we could only fly through the days on wings of surrender and trust!

Hannah Whitall Smith

—Your Thoughts for Today—

_____

_____

_____

_____

_____

_____

_____

_____

FINDING CONTENTMENT

I've learned by now to be quite content whatever my circumstances. I'm just as happy with little as with much, with much as with little. I've found the recipe for being happy whether full or hungry, hands full or hands empty.

Philippians 4:11-12 MSG

Where can we find contentment? Is it a result of wealth, or power, or beauty, or fame? Hardly. Genuine contentment is a gift from God to those who trust Him and follow His commandments.

Enduring peace is a spiritual gift from the Creator to those who obey Him and accept His will. If we don't find contentment in God, we will never find it anywhere else. But, if we seek Him and obey Him, we will be blessed with an inner peace that is beyond human understanding. When God dwells at the center of our lives, peace and contentment will belong to us just as surely as we belong to Him.

Our sense of joy, satisfaction, and fulfillment in life increases, no matter what the circumstances, if we are in the center of God's will.

Billy Graham

—Your Thoughts for Today—

NOT ENOUGH HOURS?

It is good to give thanks to the Lord, to sing praises to the Most High. It is good to proclaim your unfailing love in the morning, your faithfulness in the evening.

Psalm 92:1-2 NLT

Each day has 1,440 minutes—do you value your relationship with God enough to spend a few of those minutes with Him? He deserves that much of your time and more—is He receiving it from you? Hopefully so. But if you find that you're simply "too busy" for a daily chat with your Father in heaven, it's time to take a long, hard look at your priorities and your values.

As you consider your plans for the day ahead, here's a tip: organize your life around this simple principle: "God first." When you place your Creator where He belongs—at the very center of your day and your life—the rest of your priorities will fall into place.

I suggest you discipline yourself to spend time daily in a systematic reading of God's Word. Make this "quiet time" a priority that nobody can change.

Warren Wiersbe

—Your Thoughts for Today—

HOPE FOR THE JOURNEY

Therefore, we may boldly say: The Lord is my helper; I will not be afraid. What can man do to me?

Hebrews 13:6 Holman CSB

Because we are saved by a risen Christ, we can have hope for the future, no matter how desperate our circumstances may seem. After all, God has promised that we are His throughout eternity. And, He has told us that we must place our hopes in Him.

Today, summon the courage to follow God. Even if the path seems difficult, even if your heart is fearful, trust your Heavenly Father and follow Him. Trust Him with your day, with your life, and with your recovery. Do His work, care for His children, and share His Good News. Let Him guide your steps. He will not lead you astray.

Why rely on yourself and fall? Cast yourself upon His arm. Be not afraid. He will not let you slip. Cast yourself in confidence. He will receive you and heal you.

St. Augustine

—Your Thoughts for Today—

_____

_____

_____

_____

_____

_____

DREAM BIG

With God's power working in us, God can do much, much more than anything we can ask or imagine.

Are you willing to entertain the possibility that God has big plans in store for you? Hopefully so. Yet sometimes, especially if you've recently experienced a life-altering disappointment, you may find it difficult to envision a brighter future for yourself and your family. If so, it's time to reconsider your own capabilities . . . and God's.

Your Heavenly Father created you with unique gifts and untapped talents; your job is to tap them. When you do, you'll begin to feel an increasing sense of confidence in yourself and in your future. So even if you're experiencing difficult symptoms or difficult days, don't abandon your dreams. Instead, trust that God is preparing you for greater things.

Whatever sort of tribulation we suffer, we should always remember that its purpose is to make us spurn the present and reach out to the future.

John Calvin

—Your Thoughts for Today—

_____

_____

_____

_____

_____

WE ARE ALL ROLE MODELS

You are the light of the world. A city situated on a hill cannot be hidden. No one lights a lamp and puts it under a basket, but rather on a lampstand, and it gives light for all who are in the house. In the same way, let your light shine before men, so that they may see your good works and give glory to your Father in heaven.

Matthew 5:14-16 Holman CSB

Whether we like it or not, we are role models. Hopefully, the lives we lead and the choices we make will serve as enduring examples of the spiritual abundance that is available to all who worship God and obey His commandments.

As you move through and beyond your illness, people will be watching you. Friends will be watching you; family members will be watching; fellow patients will be watching. Will you be a positive role model? If so, congratulations. But if certain aspects of your behavior could stand improvement, the best day to begin your self-improvement regimen is this one. Because whether you realize it or not, people you love are watching your behavior, and they're learning how to live. You owe it to them—and to yourself—to live righteously and well.

More depends on my walk than my talk.

D. L. Moody

—Your Thoughts for Today—

_____

_____

_____

A LIGHT TO MY PATH

Your word is a lamp to my feet and a light to my path.
Psalm 119:105 NKJV

Are you a person who trusts God's Word without reservation? Hopefully so, because the Bible is unlike any other book—it is a guidebook for life here on earth and for life eternal. The Psalmist describes God's Word as, "a light to my path." Is the Bible your lamp? If not, you are depriving yourself of a priceless gift from the Creator.

Vance Havner observed, "It takes calm, thoughtful, prayerful meditation on the Word to extract its deepest nourishment." How true. God's Word can be a roadmap to a place of righteousness and abundance. Make it your roadmap as you travel through and beyond your illness.

God's wisdom can be a light to guide your steps. Claim it as your light today, tomorrow, and every day of your life—and then walk confidently in the footsteps of God's only begotten Son.

———

The Scriptures were not given for our information, but for our transformation.

D. L. Moody

—Your Thoughts for Today—

_____

_____

_____

_____

_____

KEEPING UP APPEARANCES

We justify our actions by appearances; God examines our motives.

Proverbs 21:2 MSG

As you make the journey through and beyond cancer, your appearance may change. If so, please remember that while the world sees you as you appear to be, God sees you as you really are. The Father sees your heart, and He understands your intentions. The opinions of others should be relatively unimportant to you. However, God's view of you—His understanding of your actions, your thoughts, and your motivations—should be vitally important.

So if your appearance begins to change, please take those changes in stride. After all, appearances change, but God's love doesn't. And His love makes all the difference.

———

Outside appearances, things like the way you look or the clothes you wear, are important to other people but totally unimportant to God. Trust God.

Jim Gallery

—Your Thoughts for Today—

_____

_____

_____

_____

_____

IN FOCUS

Let your eyes look forward; fix your gaze straight ahead.
Proverbs 4:25 Holman CSB

What is your focus today? Are you willing to focus your thoughts and energies on God's blessings and upon His will for your life? Or will you focus on your fears and doubts? This day—and every day hereafter—is a chance to celebrate the life that God has given you. It's also a chance to give thanks to the One who has offered you more blessings than you can possibly count.

Today, why not focus your thoughts on the joy that is rightfully yours in Christ? Why not take time to celebrate God's promises? Why not trust your hopes instead of your fears? When you do, you will think optimistically about yourself and your world . . . and you can then share your optimism with others. They'll be better for it, and so will you. But not necessarily in that order.

Whatever we focus on determines what we become.
E. Stanley Jones

—Your Thoughts for Today—

_____

_____

_____

_____

_____

_____

EXTREME CHANGES

Then He said to them all, "If anyone wants to come with Me, he must deny himself, take up his cross daily, and follow Me."

Luke 9:23 Holman CSB

Jesus made an extreme sacrifice for you. Are you willing to make extreme changes in your life for Him? Can you honestly say that you're passionate about your faith and that you're really following Jesus? Hopefully so. But if you're preoccupied with other things—or if you're strictly a one-day-a-week Christian—then you're in need of an extreme spiritual makeover!

Nothing is more important than your wholehearted commitment to your Creator and to His only begotten Son. Your faith must never be an afterthought; it must be your ultimate priority, your ultimate possession, and your ultimate passion. You are the recipient of Christ's love. Accept it enthusiastically and share it passionately. Jesus deserves your extreme enthusiasm; the world deserves it; and you deserve the experience of sharing it.

Jesus Christ is not a security from storms. He is perfect security in storms.

Kathy Troccoli

—Your Thoughts for Today—

_____

_____

_____

_____

BUILDING FELLOWSHIP

How good and pleasant it is when brothers can live together!
Psalm 133:1 Holman CSB

Fellowship with other believers should be an integral part of your journey back to health. Your association with fellow Christians should be uplifting, enlightening, encouraging, and consistent.

Are you an active member of your own fellowship? Are you a builder of bridges inside the four walls of your church and outside it? Do you contribute to God's glory by contributing your time and your talents to a close-knit band of believers? Hopefully so. The fellowship of believers is intended to be a powerful tool for spreading God's Good News and uplifting His children. And God intends for you to be a fully contributing member of that fellowship. Your intentions should be the same.

———

The Bible knows nothing of solitary religion.

John Wesley

—Your Thoughts for Today—

_____

_____

_____

_____

_____

_____

_____

GOD FIRST

Happy are those who fear the Lord. Yes, happy are those who delight in doing what he commands.

Psalm 112:1 NLT

One of the quickest ways to improve your day and your life—and the surest way—is to do it with God as your partner. When you put God first in every aspect of your life, you'll be comforted by the knowledge that His wisdom is the ultimate wisdom and that His plans are the right plans for you. When you put God first, your outlook will change, your priorities will change, and your behaviors will change. And, when you put Him first, you'll experience the genuine peace and lasting comfort that only He can give.

In the book of Exodus, God instructs us to place no gods before Him (20:3). Does God rule your heart? Make certain that the honest answer to this question is a resounding yes. And then prepare yourself for the cascade of spiritual and emotional blessings that are sure to follow.

When true believers are awed by the greatness of God and by the privilege of becoming His children, then they become sincerely motivated, effective evangelists.

Bill Hybels

—Your Thoughts for Today—

GOD'S GUIDANCE

The steps of a good man are ordered by the LORD.

Psalm 37:23 KJV

God is intensely interested in each of us, and He will guide our steps if we serve Him obediently. When we sincerely offer heartfelt prayers to our Heavenly Father, He will give direction and meaning to our lives—but He won't force us to follow Him. To the contrary, God has given us the free will to follow His commandments . . . or not.

Will you trust God to guide your steps? You should. When you entrust your life to Him completely and without reservation, God will give you the strength to meet any challenge, the courage to face any trial, and the wisdom to live in His righteousness and in His peace. So trust Him today and seek His guidance. When you do, your next step will be the right one.

Only He can guide you to invest your life in worthwhile ways. This guidance will come as you "walk" with Him and listen to Him.

Henry Blackaby and Claude King

—Your Thoughts for Today—

THE BREAD OF LIFE

I am the bread of life, Jesus told them. "No one who comes to Me will ever be hungry, and no one who believes in Me will ever be thirsty again."

John 6:35 Holman CSB

He was the Son of God, but He wore a crown of thorns. He was the Savior of mankind, yet He was put to death on a roughhewn cross made of wood. He offered His healing touch to an unsaved world, and yet the same hands that had healed the sick and raised the dead were pierced with nails.

Jesus Christ, the Son of God, was born into humble circumstances. He walked this earth, not as a ruler of men, but as the Savior of mankind. His crucifixion, a torturous punishment that was intended to end His life and His reign, instead became the pivotal event in the history of all humanity.

Jesus is the bread of life. Accept His grace. Share His love. And follow in His footsteps.

The crucial question for each of us is this: What do you think of Jesus, and do you yet have a personal acquaintance with Him?

Hannah Whitall Smith

—Your Thoughts for Today—

HIS HEALING TOUCH

I am the Lord that healeth thee.

As you make the harrowing journey through and beyond serious illness, there is a timeless source of comfort and assurance that is as near as your bookshelf. That source is the Holy Bible.

God's Word has much to say about every aspect of your life, including your health. And, when you face concerns of any sort, God is with you. So trust your medical doctors to do their part, but place your ultimate trust in your benevolent Heavenly Father. His healing touch, like His love, endures forever.

———

Ultimate healing and the glorification of the body are certainly among the blessings of Calvary for the believing Christian. Immediate healing is not guaranteed.

Warren Wiersbe

—Your Thoughts for Today—

_____

_____

_____

_____

_____

_____

_____

_____

CONTENTED IN HIM

The LORD will give strength to His people; the LORD will bless His people with peace.

Psalm 29:11 NKJV

Everywhere we turn, or so it seems, the world promises us contentment and happiness. But the contentment that the world offers is fleeting and incomplete. Thankfully, the contentment that God offers is all encompassing and everlasting.

Happiness depends less upon our circumstances than upon our thoughts. When we turn our thoughts to God, to His gifts, and to His glorious creation, we experience the joy that God intends for His children.

Do you sincerely want to be a contented Christian? Then set your mind and your heart upon God's love and His grace. Seek first the salvation that is available through a personal relationship with Jesus Christ, and then claim the joy, the contentment, and the spiritual abundance that the Shepherd offers His sheep.

Real contentment hinges on what's happening inside us, not around us.

Charles Stanley

—Your Thoughts for Today—

_____

_____

_____

_____

THE MIRACLE WORKER

But Jesus looked at them and said to them, "With men this is impossible, but with God all things are possible."

Matthew 19:26 NKJV

God is a miracle worker. Throughout history He has intervened in the course of human events in ways that cannot be explained by science or human rationale. And He's still doing so today.

God's miracles are not limited to special occasions, nor are they witnessed by a select few. God is crafting His wonders all around us: the miracle of the birth of a new baby; the miracle of a world renewing itself with every sunrise; the miracle of lives transformed by God's love and grace. Each day, God's handiwork is evident for all to see and experience.

Today, seize the opportunity to inspect God's hand at work. His miracles come in a variety of shapes and sizes, so keep your eyes and your heart open. Be watchful, and you'll soon be amazed.

———

Throughout history, when God's people found themselves facing impossible odds, they reminded themselves of God's limitless power.

Bill Hybels

—Your Thoughts for Today—

_____

_____

_____

_____

PROBLEMS IN PERSPECTIVE

It is important to look at things from God's point of view.
1 Corinthians 4:6 MSG

If a temporary loss of perspective has left you worried, exhausted, or both, it's time to readjust your thought patterns. Negative thoughts are habit-forming; thankfully, so are positive ones. With practice, you can form the habit of focusing on God's priorities and your possibilities. When you do, you'll soon discover that you will spend less time fretting about your challenges and more time praising God for His gifts.

When you call upon the Lord and prayerfully seek His will, He will give you wisdom and perspective. When you make God's priorities your priorities, He will direct your steps and calm your fears. So today and every day hereafter, pray for a sense of balance and perspective. And remember: no problems are too big for God—and that includes yours.

Earthly fears are no fears at all. Answer the big question of eternity, and the little questions of life fall into perspective.

Max Lucado

— Your Thoughts for Today —

_____

_____

_____

_____

_____

DEFEATING DISCOURAGEMENT

The Lord is the One who will go before you. He will be with you; He will not leave you or forsake you. Do not be afraid or discouraged.

Deuteronomy 31:8 Holman CSB

When unexpected bad news arrives at the doorstep, we may be tempted to abandon hope. Thankfully, on those cloudy days when our strength is sapped and our faith is shaken, there exists a source from which we can draw courage and wisdom. That source is God.

When we seek to form a more intimate and dynamic relationship with our Creator, He renews our spirits and restores our souls. God's promise is made clear in Isaiah 40:31: "But those who wait on the Lord shall renew their strength; they shall mount up with wings like eagles, they shall run and not be weary, they shall walk and not faint" (NKJV). And upon this promise we can—and should—depend.

We look at our burdens and heavy loads, and we shrink from them. But, if we lift them and bind them about our hearts, they become wings, and on them we can rise and soar toward God.

Mrs. Charles E. Cowman

When you accept disappointment, when you trust God, and when you yield to Him, you leave something behind to help others in the battles of life.

Warren Wiersbe

When we hit a tough spot, our tendency is to feel abandoned. In fact, just the opposite is true, for at that moment, we are more than ever the object of God's concern.

Charles Swindoll

To lose heart is to lose everything.

John Eldredge

Would we know the major chords were so sweet if there were no minor key?

Mrs. Charles E. Cowman

—Your Thoughts for Today—

AN ATTITUDE OF GRATITUDE

And let the peace of God rule in your hearts...and be ye thankful.

Colossians 3:15 KJV

For most of us, life is busy and complicated. And when we're not feeling our best, self-pity comes easily. Amid the rush and crush of the daily grind, we may lose sight of God's blessings. But, when we forget to slow down and say "Thank You" to our Maker, we rob ourselves of His presence, His peace, and His joy.

Our task, as believing Christians, is to praise God many times each day. Then, with gratitude in our hearts, we can face our daily duties with the perspective and power that only He can provide.

A spirit of thankfulness makes all the difference.

Billy Graham

—Your Thoughts for Today—

FAITH FOR YOUR JOURNEY

Everything is possible to the one who believes.

Mark 9:23 Holman CSB

When a suffering woman sought healing by merely touching the hem of His cloak, Jesus replied, "Daughter, be of good comfort; thy faith hath made thee whole" (Matthew 9:22 KJV). The message to believers of every generation is clear: we must live by faith today and every day.

How can you strengthen your faith? Through praise, through worship, through Bible study, and through prayer. And, please remember that the work required to build and sustain your faith is an ongoing process. As Corrie ten Boom noted, "Conversion is not the end of your journey—it is only the beginning."

Faith is confidence in the promises of God or confidence that God will do what He has promised.

Charles Stanley

—Your Thoughts for Today—

_____

_____

_____

_____

_____

_____

_____

ADDITIONAL RESPONSIBILITIES

So he who had received five talents came and brought five other talents, saying, "Lord, you delivered to me five talents; look, I have gained five more talents besides them." His lord said to him, "Well done, good and faithful servant; you were faithful over a few things, I will make you ruler over many things. Enter into the joy of your lord."

Matthew 25:20-21 NKJV

God has promised us this: when we do our duties in small matters, He will give us additional responsibilities. Sometimes, those responsibilities come when God changes the course of our lives so that we may better serve Him. Sometimes, our rewards come in the form of temporary setbacks that lead, in turn, to greater victories. Sometimes, God rewards us by answering "no" to our prayers so that He can say "yes" to a far grander request.

If you seek to be God's servant in great matters, be faithful, be patient, and be dutiful in smaller matters. Then step back and watch as God surprises you with the spectacular creativity of His infinite wisdom and His perfect plan.

—Your Thoughts for Today—

THE IMPORTANCE OF PRAYER

Be anxious for nothing, but in everything by prayer and supplication, with thanksgiving, let your requests be made known to God.

Philippians 4:6 NKJV

As you continue on the path toward healing, remember that prayer is not a thing to be taken lightly or used infrequently. Prayer should never be reserved for mealtimes or for bedtimes; it should be an ever-present focus throughout your day.

In his first letter to the Thessalonians, Paul wrote, "Rejoice evermore. Pray without ceasing. In every thing give thanks: for this is the will of God in Christ Jesus concerning you" (5:17-18 KJV). Paul's words apply to every Christian of every generation. So, pray constantly about things great and small. God is listening, and He wants to hear from you. Now.

———◆∙◆∙◆———

Prayer is the most important tool for your mission to the world.

Rick Warren

—Your Thoughts for Today—

_____

_____

_____

_____

_____

_____

CONSTANT PRAISE

Therefore, through Him let us continually offer up to God a sacrifice of praise, that is, the fruit of our lips that confess His name.

Hebrews 13:15 Holman CSB

The Bible makes it clear: it pays to praise God. But sometimes, when we're feeling ill or worried, we may forget to say "Thank You" to the Giver of all good gifts.

Worship and praise should be a part of everything we do. Otherwise, we quickly lose perspective as we fall prey to the demands of the moment.

Do you sincerely desire to be a worthy servant of the One who has given you eternal love and eternal life? Then praise Him for who He is and for what He has done for you. Praise Him all day long, every day, for as long as you live . . . and then for all eternity.

———————

Praise opens the window of our hearts, preparing us to walk more closely with God. Prayer raises the window of our spirit, enabling us to listen more clearly to the Father.

Max Lucado

—Your Thoughts for Today—

THE ANTIDOTE TO WORRY

Therefore don't worry about tomorrow, because tomorrow will worry about itself. Each day has enough trouble of its own.

Matthew 6:34 Holman CSB

"Worry does not empty tomorrow of its sorrow; it empties today of its strength," so writes Corrie ten Boom, a woman who survived a Nazi concentration camp during World War II. And while our own situations cannot be compared to Corrie's, we still worry about countless matters both great and small. Even though we are Christians who have been given the assurance of salvation—even though we are Christians who have received the promise of God's love and protection—we find ourselves fretting over the countless details of life.

Today, put the brakes on your worries by turning them over to a Power greater than yourself. Spend your valuable time and energy solving the problems you can solve today . . . and trust God to do the rest.

God does not promise to protect us from trials, but to protect us in trials. The dangers of life may hurt us but they can never harm us.

Warren Wiersbe

—Your Thoughts for Today—

_____

_____

_____

ONE MOUTH, TWO EARS

Everyone must be quick to hear, slow to speak, and slow to anger, for man's anger does not accomplish God's righteousness.

James 1:19-20 Holman CSB

Perhaps God gave each of us one mouth and two ears in order that we might listen twice as much as we speak. Unfortunately, many of us do otherwise, especially when we become angry.

Anger is a natural human emotion that is sometimes necessary and appropriate. Even Jesus Himself became angered when He confronted the moneychangers in the temple. But, more often than not, our frustrations are of the more mundane variety. When you are tempted to lose your temper over the minor inconveniences of life, don't. Turn away from anger, and turn instead to God.

The fire of anger, if not quenched by loving forgiveness, will spread and defile and destroy the work of God.

Warren Wiersbe

—Your Thoughts for Today—

_____

_____

_____

_____

_____

_____

_____

EXPECTING THE BEST

This is the day the Lord has made; let us rejoice and be glad in it.

Psalm 118:24 Holman CSB

What do you expect from the day ahead? Are you expecting God to do wonderful things, or are you living beneath a cloud of apprehension and doubt? The familiar words of Psalm 118:24 remind us of a profound yet simple truth: "This is the day which the LORD hath made; we will rejoice and be glad in it" (KJV).

For Christian believers, every day begins and ends with God's Son and God's promises. When we accept Christ into our hearts, God promises us the opportunity for earthly peace and spiritual abundance. But more importantly, God promises us the priceless gift of eternal life.

As we face the inevitable challenges of life-here-on-earth, we must arm ourselves with the promises of God's Holy Word. When we do, we can expect the best, not only for the day ahead, but also for all eternity.

When we meditate on God and remember the promises He has given us in His Word, our faith grows, and our fears dissolve.

Charles Stanley

—Your Thoughts for Today—

_____

_____

_____

SPREADING KINDNESS

Don't be obsessed with getting your own advantage. Forget yourselves long enough to lend a helping hand.

Philippians 2:4 MSG

The noted American theologian Phillips Brooks advised, "Be such a man, and live such a life, that if every man were such as you, and every life a life like yours, this earth would be God's Paradise." One tangible way to make the world a more godly place is to spread kindness wherever we go.

Sometimes, when we feel happy or generous, we find it easy to be kind. Other times, when we are discouraged, weary, or ill, we can scarcely summon the energy to utter a single kind word. But, God's commandment is clear: He intends that we make the conscious choice to treat others with kindness and respect, no matter our circumstances, no matter our emotions.

Today, honor Christ by following His commandment and obeying the Golden Rule. He expects no less, and He deserves no less.

We worship God through service. The authentic server views each opportunity to lead or serve as an opportunity to worship God.

Bill Hybels

—Your Thoughts for Today—

BEHAVIOR THAT IS CONSISTENT WITH YOUR BELIEFS

If the way you live isn't consistent with what you believe, then it's wrong.

Romans 14:23 MSG

In describing our beliefs, our actions are far better descriptors than our words. Yet far too many of us spend more energy talking about our beliefs than living by them—with predictably poor results.

As believers, we must beware: Our actions should always give credence to the changes that Christ can make in the lives of those who walk with Him.

Your beliefs shape your values, and your values shape your life. Is your life a clearly-crafted picture book of your creed? Are your actions always consistent with your beliefs? Are you willing to practice the philosophies that you preach? Hopefully so; otherwise, you'll be tormented by inconsistencies between your beliefs and your behaviors.

We must understand that the first and chief thing—for everyone who would do the work of Jesus—is to believe, and in doing so, to become linked to Him, the Almighty One.

Andrew Murray

—Your Thoughts for Today—

_____

_____

_____

WHEN TIMES ARE TOUGH

Then they cried out to the Lord in their trouble; He saved them from their distress.

Psalm 107:13 Holman CSB

God promises us eternal life through His Son Jesus Christ, but God does not promise us that our earthly lives will be free from pain. Instead, He promises that He will give strength to the weary and hope to those who suffer.

If you're enduring difficult days, don't give up and don't give in. Instead, turn your thoughts and your prayers to God. He promises that wherever we are, whether at the peak of the mountaintop or in the darkness of the deepest valley, He will be there also. And you can be sure that His strength is sufficient to meet—and to rise above—any challenge you face.

Suffering is never for nothing. It is that you and I might be conformed to the image of Christ.

Elisabeth Elliot

No matter how efficient, smart, or independent we happen to think ourselves to be, sooner or later we run into a brick wall that our intelligence or experience cannot handle for us. We can fake it, avoid it, or blunder through it. But, a better solution would be to find someone who has walked that way before and has gained wisdom from experience.

Gloria Gaither

Our afflictions are designed not to break us but to bend us toward the eternal and the holy.

Barbara Johnson

The sermon of your life in tough times ministers to people more powerfully than the most eloquent speaker.

Bill Bright

Despair is always the gateway of faith.

Oswald Chambers

—Your Thoughts for Today—

_____

_____

_____

_____

_____

_____

_____

_____

_____

_____

_____

_____

_____

ALWAYS HOPEFUL

Rejoice in hope; be patient in affliction; be persistent in prayer.

Romans 12:12 Holman CSB

Have you ever felt hope for the future slipping away? If so, you have temporarily lost sight of the hope that we, as believers, must place in the promises of our Heavenly Father. If you are feeling discouraged, worried, or worse, remember the words of Psalm 31: "Be of good courage, and He shall strengthen your heart."

Because we are saved by a risen Christ, we can have hope for the future, no matter how desperate our circumstances may seem. After all, God has promised that we are His throughout eternity. And, He has told us that we must place our hopes in Him.

Of course, we will face disappointments and failures, but these are only temporary defeats. Of course, this world can be a place of trials and tribulations, but we are secure. God has promised us peace, joy, and eternal life. And God keeps His promises today, tomorrow, and forever.

—Your Thoughts for Today—

WITH ALL YOUR HEART

Love the Lord your God with all your heart, with all your soul, and with all your strength.

Deuteronomy 6:5 Holman CSB

C. S. Lewis observed, "A man's spiritual health is exactly proportional to his love for God." If we are to enjoy the spiritual health that God intends for us, we must praise Him, we must love Him, and we must obey Him.

When we worship God faithfully and obediently, we invite His love into our hearts. When we truly worship God, we allow Him to rule over our days and our lives. In turn, we grow to love God even more deeply as we sense His love for us.

Today, open your heart to the Father. And let your obedience be a fitting response to His never-ending love.

———

I love Him because He first loved me, and He still does love me, and He will love me forever and ever.

Bill Bright

—Your Thoughts for Today—

_____

_____

_____

_____

_____

_____

WHERE TO FIND HELP

I raise my eyes toward the mountains. Where will my help come from? My help comes from the Lord, the Maker of heaven and earth. He will not allow your foot to slip; your Protector will not slumber. Indeed, the Protector of Israel does not slumber or sleep. The Lord protects you; the Lord is a shelter right by your side. The sun will not strike you by day, or the moon by night. The Lord will protect you from all harm; He will protect your life. The Lord will protect your coming and going both now and forever.

Psalm 121 Holman CSB

Eugene Peterson observed, "The promise of Psalm 121 is not that we shall never stub our toes, but that no injury, no illness, no accident, no distress will have evil power over us, that is, will be able to separate us from God's purposes in us." Wherever you find yourself today, remember that your help comes from God. Always from God.

—Your Thoughts for Today—

_____

_____

_____

_____

_____

_____

PLEASING GOD

But neither exile nor homecoming is the main thing. Cheerfully pleasing God is the main thing, and that's what we aim to do, regardless of our conditions.

2 Corinthians 5:9 MSG

Whom will you try to please today: God or man? Your primary obligation is not to please imperfect men and women. Your obligation is to strive diligently to meet the expectations of an all-knowing and perfect God.

Sometimes, because you're an imperfect human being, you may become so wrapped up in meeting society's expectations that you fail to focus on God's expectations. To do so is a mistake of major proportions—don't make it. Instead, seek God's guidance as you focus your energies on becoming the best "you" that you can possibly be. And, when it comes to matters of conscience, seek approval not from your peers, but from your Creator.

Make God's will the focus of your life day by day. If you seek to please Him and Him alone, you'll find yourself satisfied with life.

Kay Arthur

—Your Thoughts for Today—

_____

_____

_____

_____

HOPE AND HAPPINESS

Happy is the one whose help is the God of Jacob, whose hope is in the Lord his God.

Psalm 146:5 Holman CSB

Hope and happiness are traveling companions. After all, God is good; His love endures; and we have every reason to be hopeful. But sometimes, in life's darker moments, you may lose sight of these blessings, and when you do, it's easy to lose hope. Yet if you sincerely desire to lead happier, healthier lives, you will learn to live by faith.

Are you a hope-filled Christian? You should be. You have an array of talents within you and an assortment of opportunities before you. You have the potential to achieve your goals and the wherewithal to accomplish your dreams. So remember the words of Maya Angelou, who observed, "The horizon leans forward, offering you space to place new steps of change." Then, step toward your horizon with assurance and hope . . . it's the happy—and healthy—way to live.

Never yield to gloomy anticipation. Place your hope and confidence in God. He has no record of failure.

Mrs. Charles E. Cowman

The Lord Himself has laid the foundation of His people's hopes. We must determine if our hopes are built on this foundation.

C. H. Spurgeon

Oh, remember this: There is never a time when we may not hope in God. Whatever our necessities, however great our difficulties, and though to all appearance, help is impossible, yet our business is to hope in God, and it will be found that it is not in vain.

George Mueller

Faith looks back and draws courage; hope looks ahead and keeps desire alive.

John Eldredge

Our hope in Christ for the future is the mainstream of our joy.

C. H. Spurgeon

—Your Thoughts for Today—

MADE WHOLE

But Jesus turned him about, and when he saw her, he said, Daughter, be of good comfort; thy faith hath made thee whole. And the woman was made whole from that hour.

Matthew 9:22 KJV

Until we have been touched by the Savior, we can never be completely whole. Until we have placed our hearts and our lives firmly in the hands of the living Christ, we are incomplete. Until we come to know Jesus, we long for a sense of peace that continues to elude us no matter how diligently we search.

It is only through God that we discover genuine peace. We can search far and wide for worldly substitutes, but when we seek peace apart from God, we will find neither peace nor God.

As believers, we are invited to accept the "peace that passes all understanding" (Philippians 4:7 NIV). That peace, of course, is God's peace. Let us accept His peace, and let us share it today, tomorrow, and every day that we live.

Whoever you are, whatever your condition or circumstance, whatever your past or problem, Jesus can restore you to wholeness.

Anne Graham Lotz

—Your Thoughts for Today—

_____

_____

_____

ASKING FOR DIRECTIONS

Now if any of you lacks wisdom, he should ask God, who gives to all generously and without criticizing, and it will be given to him.

James 1:5 Holman CSB

Jesus made it clear to His disciples: they should petition God to meet their needs. So should we. Genuine, heartfelt prayer produces powerful changes in us and in our world. When we lift our hearts to God, we open ourselves to a never-ending source of divine wisdom and infinite love.

Do you have questions about your illness that you simply can't answer? Do you have needs that you simply can't meet by yourself? Do you sincerely seek to know God's unfolding plans for your life? If so, ask Him for direction, for protection, and for strength—and then keep asking Him every day that you live. Whatever your need, no matter how great or small, pray about it and never lose hope. God is not just near; He is here, and He's perfectly capable of answering your prayers. Now, it's up to you to ask.

—Your Thoughts for Today—

_____

_____

_____

_____

_____

LIMITLESS POWER,
LIMITLESS LOVE

I pray that the eyes of your heart may be enlightened so you may know what is the hope of His calling, what are the glorious riches of His inheritance among the saints, and what is the immeasurable greatness of His power to us who believe, according to the working of His vast strength.

Ephesians 1:18-19 Holman CSB

Because God's power is limitless, it is far beyond the comprehension of mortal minds. Yet even though we cannot fully understand the awesome power of God, we can praise it. When we worship God with faith and assurance, when we place Him at the absolute center of our lives, we invite His love into our hearts. In turn, we grow to love Him more deeply as we sense His love for us. St. Augustine wrote, "I love you, Lord, not doubtingly, but with absolute certainty. Your Word beat upon my heart until I fell in love with you, and now the universe and everything in it tells me to love you."

Let us pray that we, too, will turn our hearts to the Creator, knowing with certainty that His heart has ample room for each of us, and that we, in turn, must make room in our hearts for Him.

—Your Thoughts for Today—

HOPE IS CONTAGIOUS

Finally, all of you be of one mind, having compassion for one another; love as brothers, be tenderhearted, be courteous.
1 Peter 3:8 NKJV

One of the reasons that God placed you here on earth is so that you might become a beacon of encouragement to people in need. As a faithful follower of the One from Galilee, you have every reason to be hopeful, and you have every reason to share your hopes with others. When you do, you will discover that hope, like other human emotions, is contagious.

Today, as you make the journey through and beyond cancer, choose your words carefully so as to build others up through wholesome, honest encouragement. Look for the good in others and celebrate the good that you find. When you do, you'll be a powerful force of encouragement to your friends and family…and a worthy servant to your God.

He climbs highest who helps another up.

Zig Ziglar

—Your Thoughts for Today—

BEYOND GRIEF

The Lord shall give thee rest from thy sorrow, and from thy fear....

Isaiah 14:3 KJV

Grief is a uniquely personal experience. But grief is also a universal experience, a journey that has been clearly mapped by those who have documented the common elements of human suffering.

Grief usually begins with shock and then gives way to intense pain. Over time, as the mourner regains his or her emotional balance, the pain begins to fade. Gradually, a new life is raised from the ashes of the old. Christians face grief armed with God's promises. Through the Holy Bible, He promises to comfort and heal those who call upon Him.

So as you move through and beyond your illness, be hopeful. God is with you, God is good, and you are protected.

The strength that we claim from God's Word does not depend on circumstances. Circumstances will be difficult, but our strength will be sufficient.

Corrie ten Boom

—Your Thoughts for Today—

_____

_____

_____

_____

_____

SEEKING SOUND ADVICE

Arrogance leads to nothing but strife, but wisdom is gained by those who take advice.

Proverbs 13:10 Holman CSB

As you make the journey through and beyond your illness, it's so important to find friends, mentors, and physicians whose advice you can trust. And then, once you've received their advice, you should be wise enough to take it.

Are you walking with the wise? Are you seeking advice from people you trust and admire? Do you have a team of doctors and friends who can help you and guide you? Hopefully so.

Consider your mentors to be gifts from God. Listen to them; learn from them; and be thankful for their wisdom.

It takes a wise person to give good advice, but an even wiser person to take it.

Marie T. Freeman

—Your Thoughts for Today—

_____

_____

_____

_____

_____

_____

INFINITE FORGIVENESS

*And forgive us our sins, for we ourselves also forgive everyone
in debt to us.*

Luke 11:4 NKJV

God's power to forgive, like His love, is infinite.
Despite your shortcomings, despite your sins,
God offers you immediate forgiveness and eternal life when you accept Christ as your Savior.

As a believer who is the recipient of God's forgiveness, how should you behave towards others? Should you
forgive them (just as God has forgiven you), or should
you remain embittered and resentful? The answer, of
course, is found in God's Word: you are instructed to
forgive others. When you do, you not only obey God's
command, you also free yourself from a prison of your
own making.

As you have received the mercy of God by the forgiveness
of sin and the promise of eternal life, thus you must show
mercy.

Billy Graham

—Your Thoughts for Today—

ENTHUSIASM FOR CHRIST

So roll up your sleeves, put your mind in gear, be totally ready to receive the gift that's coming when Jesus arrives. Don't lazily slip back into those old grooves of evil, doing just what you feel like doing. You didn't know any better then; you do now. As obedient children, let yourselves be pulled into a way of life shaped by God's life, a life energetic and blazing with holiness.

1 Peter 1:13-15 MSG

John Wesley advised, "Catch on fire with enthusiasm and people will come for miles to watch you burn." His words still ring true. When we fan the flames of enthusiasm for Christ, our faith serves as a beacon to others.

Your family and friends desperately need positive role models, faithful believers who share the Good News of Jesus with joyful exuberance. Be such a believer. The world desperately needs your enthusiasm—now!

———

Enthusiasm, like the flu, is contagious—we get it from one another.

Barbara Johnson

—Your Thoughts for Today—

_____

_____

_____

_____

_____

CHEERFULNESS 101

A miserable heart means a miserable life; a cheerful heart fills the day with a song.

Proverbs 15:15 MSG

Few things in life are more sad, or, for that matter, more absurd, than a grumpy Christian. Christ promises us lives of abundance and joy, but He does not force His joy upon us. We must claim His joy for ourselves, and when we do, Jesus, in turn, fills our spirits with His power and His love.

How can we receive from Christ the joy that is rightfully ours? By giving Him what is rightfully His: our hearts and our souls. When we earnestly commit ourselves to the Savior of mankind, when we place Jesus at the center of our lives and trust Him as our personal Savior, He will transform us, not just for today, but for all eternity.

———

Be assured, my dear friend, that it is no joy to God in seeing you with a dreary countenance.

C. H. *Spurgeon*

—Your Thoughts for Today—

_____

_____

_____

_____

_____

_____

GOD IS HERE

Draw near to God, and He will draw near to you.

James 4:8 Holman CSB

God is constantly making Himself available to you; therefore, when you approach Him obediently and sincerely, you will most certainly find Him: God is always available to you. Whenever it seems to you that God is distant, disinterested, or altogether absent, you may rest assured that your feelings are a reflection of your own emotional state, not an indication of God's absence.

If, during life's darker days, you seek to establish a closer relationship with Him, you can do so because God is not just near, He is here.

───◦•◦───

We look for visions of heaven, but we never dream that, all the time, God is in the commonplace things and people around us.

Oswald Chambers

—Your Thoughts for Today—

_____

_____

_____

_____

_____

_____

_____

INFINITE LOVE

For I am persuaded that neither death nor life, nor angels nor rulers, nor things present, nor things to come, nor powers, nor height, nor depth, nor any other created thing will have the power to separate us from the love of God that is in Christ Jesus our Lord!

Romans 8:38-39 Holman CSB

Christ's love for you is personal. He loves you so much that He gave His life in order that you might spend all eternity with Him. Christ loves you individually and intimately; His is a love unbounded by time or circumstance. Are you willing to experience an intimate relationship with Him? Your Savior is waiting patiently; don't make Him wait a single minute longer. Embrace His love today.

If you come to Christ, you will always have the option of an ever-present friend. You don't have to dial long-distance. He'll be with you every step of the way.

Bill Hybels

—Your Thoughts for Today—

YOUR ETERNAL JOURNEY

For this is the will of My Father: that everyone who sees the Son and believes in Him may have eternal life, and I will raise him up on the last day.

John 6:40 Holman CSB

Eternal life is not an event that begins when you die. Eternal life begins when you invite Jesus into your heart right here on earth. So it's important to remember that God's plans for you are not limited to the ups and downs of everyday life. If you've allowed Jesus to reign over your heart, you've already begun your eternal journey.

Today, give praise to the Creator for His priceless gift, the gift of eternal life. And then, when you've offered Him your thanks and your praise, share His Good News with all who cross your path.

———

Teach us to set our hopes on heaven, to hold firmly to the promise of eternal life, so that we can withstand the struggles and storms of this world.

Max Lucado

—Your Thoughts for Today—

_____

_____

_____

_____

_____

_____

SEEKING GOD AND FINDING HAPPINESS

Happy is the one whose help is the God of Jacob, whose hope is in the Lord his God.

Psalm 146:5 Holman CSB

Happiness depends less upon our circumstances than upon our thoughts. When we turn our thoughts to God, to His gifts, and to His glorious creation, we experience the joy that God intends for His children. But, when we focus on the negative aspects of life, we suffer needlessly.

Do you sincerely want to be a happy Christian in good times and hard times? Then set your mind and your heart upon God's love and His grace. The fullness of life in Christ is available to all who seek it and claim it. Count yourself among that number. Seek first the salvation that is available through a personal relationship with Jesus Christ, and then claim the joy, the peace, and the spiritual abundance that the Shepherd offers His sheep.

God has charged Himself with full responsibility for our eternal happiness and stands ready to take over the management of our lives the moment we turn in faith to Him.

A. W. Tozer

—Your Thoughts for Today—

_____

_____

_____

THE SELF-FULFILLING PROPHECY

May He grant you according to your heart's desire, and fulfill all your purpose.

Psalm 20:4 NKJV

The self-fulfilling prophecy is alive, well, and living at your house. If you trust God and have faith for the future, your optimistic beliefs will give you direction and motivation. That's one reason that you should never lose hope, but certainly not the only reason. The primary reason that you, as a believer, should never lose hope, is because of God's unfailing promises.

Make no mistake about it: thoughts are powerful things: your thoughts have the power to lift you up or to hold you down. When you acquire the habit of hopeful thinking, you will have acquired a powerful tool for improving your life. So if you fall into the habit of negative thinking, think again. After all, God's Word teaches us that Christ can overcome every difficulty. And when God makes a promise, He keeps it.

People are genuinely motivated by hope and a part of that hope is the assurance of future glory with God for those who are His people.

Warren Wiersbe

—Your Thoughts for Today—

_____

_____

_____

COMPASSIONATE CHRISTIANITY

Therefore, God's chosen ones, holy and loved, put on heartfelt compassion, kindness, humility, gentleness, and patience.

Colossians 3:12 Holman CSB

The instructions of Colossians 3:12 are unambiguous: as Christians, we are to be compassionate, humble, gentle, and kind. But sometimes, we fall short. When we're ill, or exhausted, or both, we may neglect to share a kind word or a kind deed. This oversight hurts others, but it hurts us, too.

Today, slow yourself down and be alert for those who need your smile, your kind words, or your helping hand. Make kindness a centerpiece of your dealings with others. They will be blessed, and you will be too. Today, honor Christ by obeying His Golden Rule. He deserves no less, and neither, for that matter, do your friends.

———

Be so preoccupied with good will that you haven't room for ill will.

E. Stanley Jones

—Your Thoughts for Today—

_____

_____

_____

_____

_____

OBEY AND BE BLESSED

Now by this we know that we know Him, if we keep His commandments.

1 John 2:3 NKJV

God gave us His commandments for a reason: so that we might obey them and be blessed. Oswald Chambers, the author of the Christian classic devotional text, *My Utmost for His Highest*, advised, "Never support an experience which does not have God as its source, and faith in God as its result." These words serve as a powerful reminder that, as Christians, we are called to walk with God and obey His commandments. But, we live in a world that presents us with countless temptations to stray far from God's path. We Christians, when confronted with sin, have clear instructions: Walk—or better yet run—in the opposite direction.

God meant that we adjust to the Gospel—not the other way around.

Vance Havner

—Your Thoughts for Today—

NEW BEGINNINGS

I will give you a new heart and put a new spirit within you.
Ezekiel 36:26 Holman CSB

I s there some aspect of your life you'd like to change. If so, remember this simple rule: Lasting change doesn't occur "out there"; it occurs "in here." Genuine personal transformation occurs, not in the shifting sands of our own particular circumstances, but in the quiet depths of our own hearts.

Are you in search of a new beginning or, for that matter, a new you? If so, don't expect changing circumstances to miraculously transform you into the person you want to become. Transformation starts with God, and it starts in the silent center of a humble human heart—like yours.

God is not running an antique shop! He is making all things new!

Vance Havner

—Your Thoughts for Today—

_____

_____

_____

_____

_____

_____

BELIEVING MAKES
A DIFFERENCE

You love Him, though you have not seen Him. And though not seeing Him now, you believe in Him and rejoice with inexpressible and glorious joy, because you are receiving the goal of your faith, the salvation of your souls.

1 Peter 1:8-9 Holman CSB

If you'd like to partake in the peace that only God can give, make certain that your actions are guided by His Word. And while you're at it, pay careful attention to the conscience that God, in His infinite wisdom, has placed in your heart. Don't treat your faith as if it were separate from your everyday life. Weave your beliefs into the very fabric of your day. When you do, God will honor your good works, and your good works will honor God.

If you seek to be a responsible believer, you must realize that it is never enough to hear the instructions of God; you must also live by them. And it is never enough to wait idly by while others do God's work here on earth; you, too, must act. Doing God's work is a responsibility that every Christian (including you) should bear. And when you do, your loving Heavenly Father will reward your efforts with a bountiful harvest.

—Your Thoughts for Today—

A PASSIONATE PURSUIT OF
GOD'S TRUTH

But grow in the grace and knowledge of our Lord and Savior Jesus Christ. To Him be the glory both now and forever. Amen.

2 Peter 3:18 NKJV

Have you established a passionate relationship with God's Holy Word? Hopefully so. The words of Matthew 4:4 remind us that, "Man shall not live by bread alone but by every word that proceedeth out of the mouth of God" (KJV). As believers, we must study the Bible and meditate upon its meaning for our lives. Otherwise, we deprive ourselves of a priceless gift from our Creator.

Martin Luther observed, "The Bible is alive, it speaks to me; it has feet, it runs after me; it has hands, it lays hold of me. The Bible is not antique or modern. It is eternal." God's Holy Word is, indeed, an eternal, transforming, one-of-a-kind treasure. And, a passing acquaintance with the Good Book is insufficient for Christians who seek to obey God's Word and to understand His will—passionate believers must never live by bread alone . . .

—Your Thoughts for Today—

COURAGE FOR YOUR JOURNEY

Therefore don't worry about tomorrow, because tomorrow will worry about itself. Each day has enough trouble of its own.

Matthew 6:34 Holman CSB

Are you anxious about situations that you cannot control? Take your anxieties to God. Are you troubled about changes that threaten to disrupt your life? Take your troubles to Him. Does your corner of the world seem to be trembling beneath your feet? Seek protection from the One who cannot be moved.

The same God who created the universe will protect you if you ask Him . . . so ask Him . . . and then serve Him with willing hands and a trusting heart. And rest assured that the world may change moment by moment, but God's love endures—unfathomable and unchanging—forever.

———

When we are young, change is a treat, but as we grow older, change becomes a threat. But when Jesus Christ is in control of your life, you need never fear change or decay.

Warren Wiersbe

—Your Thoughts for Today—

CHOOSING WISELY

But the wisdom that is from above is first pure, then peaceable, gentle, willing to yield, full of mercy and good fruits, without partiality and without hypocrisy.

James 3:17 NKJV

Because we are creatures of free will, we make choices—lots of them. When we make choices that are pleasing to our Heavenly Father, we are blessed. When we make choices that cause us to walk in the footsteps of God's Son, we enjoy the abundance that Christ has promised to those who follow Him. But when make choices that are displeasing to God, we sow seeds that have the potential to bring forth a bitter harvest.

Today, as you encounter the challenges of every-day living, you will make hundreds of choices. Choose wisely. Make your thoughts and your actions pleasing to God. And remember: every choice that is displeasing to Him is the wrong choice—no exceptions.

Good and evil both increase at compound interest. That is why the little decisions you and I make every day are of such infinite importance.

C. S. Lewis

—Your Thoughts for Today—

_____

_____

_____

_____

_____

HIS POWER AND YOURS

I assure you: The one who believes in Me will also do the works that I do. And he will do even greater works than these, because I am going to the Father. Whatever you ask in My name, I will do it, so that the Father may be glorified in the Son. If you ask Me anything in My name, I will do it.

John 14:12-14 Holman CSB

When you invite Christ to rule over your heart, you avail yourself of His power. And make no mistake about it: You and Christ, working together, can do miraculous things. In fact, miraculous things are exactly what Christ intends for you to do, but He won't force you to do great things on His behalf. The decision to become a full-fledged participant in His power is a decision that you must make for yourself.

The words of John 14:12-14 make this promise: when you put absolute faith in Christ, you can share in His power. Today, trust the Savior's promise and expect a miracle in His name.

The Christian life is not simply following principles but being empowered to fulfill our purpose: knowing and exalting Christ.

Franklin Graham

—Your Thoughts for Today—

_____

_____

_____

_____

COMPASSIONATE SERVANTS

Finally, all of you be of one mind, having compassion for one another; love as brothers, be tenderhearted, be courteous.

1 Peter 3:8 NKJV

God's Word commands us to be compassionate, generous servants to those who need our support. As believers, we have been richly blessed by our Creator. We, in turn, are called to share our gifts, our possessions, our testimonies, and our talents.

Concentration camp survivor Corrie ten Boom correctly observed, "The measure of a life is not its duration but its donation." These words remind us that the quality of our lives is determined not by what we are able to take from others, but instead by what we are able to share with others.

The thread of compassion is woven into the very fabric of Christ's teachings. If we are to be disciples of Christ, we, too, must be zealous in caring for others, even when we ourselves are under the care of others. Even when we are ill, we can be compassionate. And we should be. Our Savior expects no less from us. And He deserves no less.

───

When action-oriented compassion is absent, it's a telltale sign that something's spiritually amiss.

Bill Hybels

—Your Thoughts for Today—

WALKING WITH GOD

The Lord is for me; I will not be afraid. What can man do to me?

Psalm 118:6 Holman CSB

Are you tired? Discouraged? Fearful? Be comforted. Take a walk with God. Jesus called upon believers to walk with Him, and He promised them that He would teach them how to live freely and lightly (Matthew 11:28-30). Are you worried or anxious? Be confident in God's power. He will never desert you. Do you see no hope for the future? Be courageous and call upon God. He will protect you and then use you according to His purposes. Are you grieving? Know that God hears your suffering. He will comfort you and, in time, He will dry your tears. Are you confused? Listen to the quiet voice of your Heavenly Father. He is not a God of confusion. Talk with Him; listen to Him; follow His commandments. He is steadfast, and He is your Protector . . . forever.

It may be the most difficult time of your life. You may be enduring your own whirlwind. But the whirlwind is a temporary experience. Your faithful, caring Lord will see you through.

Charles Swindoll

—Your Thoughts for Today—

_____

_____

_____

A BOOK UNLIKE ANY OTHER

For I am not ashamed of the gospel, because it is God's power for salvation to everyone who believes.

Romans 1:16 Holman CSB

God's Word is unlike any other book. A. W. Tozer wrote, "The purpose of the Bible is to bring men to Christ, to make them holy and prepare them for heaven. In this it is unique among books, and it always fulfills its purpose."

George Mueller observed, "The vigor of our spiritual lives will be in exact proportion to the place held by the Bible in our lives and in our thoughts." As Christians, we are called upon to study God's Holy Word and then to share it with the world.

As you make the journey through and beyond your illness, use the Bible as your roadmap. When you do, you'll never stay lost for long.

The Bible is God's Word, given to us by God Himself so we can know Him and His will for our lives.

Billy Graham

—Your Thoughts for Today—

_____

_____

_____

_____

_____

_____

ACKNOWLEDGING YOUR BLESSINGS

The Lord bless you and keep you; the Lord make His face shine upon you, and be gracious to you.

Numbers 6:24-25 NKJV

Today, you will take one more step on your journey through and beyond your illness. Today offers one more opportunity to be genuinely thankful for your blessings. The coming day is a canvass upon which you can compose a beautiful work of art if you choose to do so.

Norman Vincent Peale observed, "The life of stress is difficult. But the life of thanksgiving—a life that comes from a positive attitude—is the easiest type of existence." And those words apply to you.

So today, even if you're weak or worried, look for things to be thankful for. If you look carefully, you won't need to look very far. And remember: when it comes time to count your blessings, nobody can count them for you.

Get rich quick. Count your blessings!

Anonymous

—Your Thoughts for Today—

_____

_____

_____

_____

_____

MID-COURSE CORRECTIONS

The sensible see danger and take cover; the foolish keep going and are punished.

Proverbs 27:12 Holman CSB

I n our fast-paced world, life has become an exercise in managing change. Our circumstances change; our relationships change; our bodies change; our health changes. We grow older every day, as does our world. Thankfully, God does not change. He is eternal, as are the truths that are found in His Holy Word.

As you make the journey through and beyond cancer, you may be facing one of life's inevitable "mid-course corrections." If so, you must place your faith, your trust, and your life in the hands of the One who does not change: your Heavenly Father. He is the unmoving rock upon which you must construct this day and every day. When you do, you are secure.

———————

With God, it isn't who you were that matters; it's who you are becoming.

Liz Curtis Higgs

—Your Thoughts for Today—

_____

_____

_____

_____

_____

_____

CHARACTER COUNTS

I have fought the good fight, I have finished the race, I have kept the faith.

2 Timothy 4:7 Holman CSB

Character is built slowly over a lifetime. It is the sum of every right decision, every honest word, every noble thought, and every heartfelt prayer. It is forged on the anvil of honorable work and polished by the twin virtues of generosity and humility. Character is a precious thing—difficult to build but easy to tear down. As believers in Christ, we must seek to live each day with discipline, honesty, and faith. When we do, character builds strength and strength builds perseverance. And perseverance makes all the difference when times are tough.

God cannot build character without our cooperation. If we resist Him, then He chastens us into submission. But, if we submit to Him, then He can accomplish His work.

Warren Wiersbe

—Your Thoughts for Today—

_____

_____

_____

_____

_____

_____

SOLVING THE RIDDLES

If you need wisdom—if you want to know what God wants you to do—ask him, and he will gladly tell you. He will not resent your asking.

James 1:5 NLT

On the road to recovery, you may have any number of questions, conundrums, and doubts. Thankfully, these riddles will be easier to solve if you look for answers in the right places. When you have questions, you should consult God's Word, you should seek the guidance of the Holy Spirit, and you should trust the counsel of your physicians and your family members.

Are you facing a difficult decision? Take your concerns to God and avail yourself of the mentors He has placed along your path. When you do, God will speak to you in His own way and in His own time, and when He does, you can most certainly trust the answers that He gives.

———

God does not give His counsel to the curious or the careless; He reveals His will to the concerned and to the consecrated.

Warren Wiersbe

—Your Thoughts for Today—

_____

_____

_____

_____

GOD'S ASSURANCE

I've told you all this so that trusting me, you will be unshakable and assured, deeply at peace. In this godless world you will continue to experience difficulties. But take heart! I've conquered the world.

John 16:33 MSG

Are you a confident believer, or do you live under a cloud of uncertainty and doubt? As a Christian, you have many reasons to be confident. After all, God is in His heaven; Christ has risen; and you are the recipient of God's grace. Despite these blessings, you may, from time to time, find yourself being tormented by negative emotions—and you are certainly not alone.

Even the most faithful Christians are overcome by occasional bouts of fear and doubt. You are no different.

But even when you feel very distant from God, remember that God is never distant from you. When you sincerely seek His presence, He will touch your heart, calm your fears, and restore your confidence.

Believe and do what God says. The life-changing consequences will be limitless, and the results will be confidence and peace of mind.

Franklin Graham

—Your Thoughts for Today—

_____

_____

_____

MEASURING YOUR WORDS

The heart of the wise teaches his mouth, and adds learning to his lips.

Proverbs 16:23 NKJV

God's Word reminds us that "Reckless words pierce like a sword, but the tongue of the wise brings healing" (Proverbs 12:18 NIV). If you seek to be a source of encouragement to friends, to family members and to fellow patients, then you must measure your words carefully. And that's exactly what God wants you to do.

Today, make this promise to yourself: vow to be an honest, effective, encouraging communicator at home, at church, at work, and everyplace in between. Speak wisely, not impulsively. Use words of kindness and praise, not words of anger or derision. Learn how to be truthful without being cruel. Remember that you have the power to heal others or to injure them, to lift others up or to hold them back. And when you learn how to lift them up, you'll soon discover that you've lifted yourself up, too.

We should ask ourselves three things before we speak: Is it true? Is it kind? Does it glorify God?

Billy Graham

—Your Thoughts for Today—

_____

_____

_____

SELF-ESTEEM ACCORDING TO GOD

For you made us only a little lower than God, and you crowned us with glory and honor.

Psalm 8:5 NLT

What are you telling yourself about yourself? When you look in the mirror, are you staring back at your biggest booster or your harshest critic? If you can learn to give yourself the benefit of the doubt—if you can learn how to have constructive conversations with the person you see in the mirror—then your self-respect will tend to take care of itself. But, if you're constantly berating yourself—if you're constantly telling yourself that you can't measure up—then you'll find that self-respect is always in short supply.

So the next time you find yourself being critical of the person you see in the mirror, ask yourself if the criticism is really valid. If it is valid, make changes . . . if not, lighten up.

The Creator has made us each one of a kind. There is nobody else exactly like us, and there never will be. Each of us is his special creation and is alive for a distinctive purpose.

Luci Swindoll

—Your Thoughts for Today—

_____

_____

_____

SEEKING HIS WILL

Teach me to do Your will, for You are my God; Your Spirit is good. Lead me in the land of uprightness.

Psalm 143:10 NKJV

God has a plan for our world and our lives. God does not do things by accident; He is willful and intentional. Unfortunately for us, we cannot always understand the will of God. Why? Because we are mortal beings with limited understanding. Although we cannot fully comprehend the will of God, we should always trust the will of God.

As this day unfolds, seek God's will and obey His Word. When you entrust your life to Him without reservation, He will give you the courage to meet any challenge, the strength to endure any trial, and the wisdom to live in His righteousness and in His peace.

I believe that in every time and place it is within our power to acquiesce in the will of God—and what peace it brings to do so!

Elisabeth Elliot

—Your Thoughts for Today—

_____

_____

_____

_____

_____

_____

STRENGTH FOR THE DAY

I can do all things through Christ which strengtheneth me.
Philippians 4:13 KJV

Have you made God the cornerstone of your life, or is He relegated to a few hours on Sunday morning? Have you genuinely allowed God to reign over every corner of your heart, or have you attempted to place Him in a spiritual compartment? The answer to these questions will determine the direction of your day and your life.

God loves you. In times of trouble, He will comfort you; in times of sorrow, He will dry your tears. When you are weak or sorrowful, God is as near as your next breath. He stands at the door of your heart and waits. Welcome Him in and allow Him to rule. And then, accept the peace, and the strength, and the protection, and the abundance that only God can give.

The knowledge that we are never alone calms the troubled sea of our lives and speaks peace to our souls.

A. W. Tozer

—Your Thoughts for Today—

_____

_____

_____

_____

_____

_____

PERFECT WISDOM

Therefore, everyone who hears these words of Mine and acts on them will be like a sensible man who built his house on the rock. The rain fell, the rivers rose, and the winds blew and pounded that house. Yet it didn't collapse, because its foundation was on the rock.

Matthew 7:24-25 Holman CSB

Where will you place your trust today? Will you trust in the wisdom of fallible men and women, or will you place your faith in God's perfect wisdom? Where you choose to place your trust will determine the direction and quality of your life.

Are you tired? Discouraged? Fearful? Be comforted and trust God. Are you worried or anxious? Be confident in God's power and trust His Holy Word. Are you confused? Listen to the quiet voice of your Heavenly Father. He is not a God of confusion. Talk with Him; listen to Him; trust Him. He is steadfast, and He is your protector . . . today, tomorrow, and forever.

If you lack knowledge, go to school. If you lack wisdom, get on your knees.

Vance Havner

—Your Thoughts for Today—

_____

_____

_____

_____

YOUR REAL RICHES

Naked I came from my mother's womb, and naked I will leave this life. The Lord gives, and the Lord takes away. Praise the name of the Lord.

Job 1:21 Holman CSB

M artin Luther observed, "Many things I have tried to grasp and have lost. That which I have placed in God's hands I still have." How true. Earthly riches are transitory; spiritual riches are not.

In our demanding world, financial security can be a good thing, but spiritual prosperity is profoundly more important. Certainly we all need the basic necessities of life, but once we've acquired those necessities, enough is enough. Why? Because our real riches are not of this world. We are never really rich until we are rich in spirit.

Here's a simple test: If you can see it, it's not going to last. The things that last are the things you cannot see.

Dennis Swanberg

—Your Thoughts for Today—

BEING A GOOD SAMARITAN

Then a Samaritan traveling down the road came to where the hurt man was. When he saw the man, he felt very sorry for him. The Samaritan went to him, poured olive oil and wine on his wounds, and bandaged them. Then he put the hurt man on his own donkey and took him to an inn where he cared for him.

Luke 10:33-34 NCV

Jesus told the story of the "Good Samaritan," a man who helped a fellow traveler when no one else would. We, too, have opportunities to be good Samaritans when we find people who need our help.

But what if you're the one who's suffering through tough times? Is there anything you can do? The answer, of course, is a resounding yes. You can start by making your own corner of the world a little nicer place to live (by sharing kind words, frequent smiles, helping hands, and heartfelt hugs). And then, you can take your concerns to God in prayer. Whether you've offered a helping hand or a heartfelt prayer, you've done a lot.

Do all the good you can. By all the means you can. In all the ways you can. In all the places you can. At all the times you can. To all the people you can. As long as ever you can.

John Wesley

—Your Thoughts for Today—

_____

_____

_____

GOD'S LESSONS

Listen to counsel and receive instruction so that you may be wise in later life.

Proverbs 19:20 Holman CSB

Have you experienced a recent setback? If so, look for the lesson that God is trying to teach you. Instead of complaining about your sad state of affairs, learn what needs to be learned, change what needs to be changed, and move on.

For most of us, it isn't very easy to discern God's lessons from the experiences of everyday life, yet learn them we must. The goal, of course, should be to learn those lessons sooner rather than later because the sooner we do, the sooner God can move on to the next lesson and the next, and the next . . .

When you persevere through a trial, God gives you a special measure of insight.

Charles Swindoll

—Your Thoughts for Today—

CONTENTMENT THAT LASTS

But godliness with contentment is a great gain. For we brought nothing into the world, and we can take nothing out. But if we have food and clothing, we will be content with these. But those who want to be rich fall into temptation, a trap, and many foolish and harmful desires, which plunge people into ruin and destruction.

1 Timothy 6:6-9 Holman CSB

The preoccupation with happiness and contentment is an ever-present theme in the modern world. We are bombarded with messages that tell us where to find peace and pleasure in a world that worships materialism and wealth. But, lasting contentment is not found in material possessions; genuine contentment is a spiritual gift from God to those who trust in Him and follow His commandments. When God dwells at the center of our lives, peace and contentment will belong to us just as surely as we belong to God.

The happiness which brings enduring worth to life is not the superficial happiness that is dependent on circumstances. It is the happiness and contentment that fills the soul in the midst of the most distressing of circumstances.

Billy Graham

—Your Thoughts for Today—

NEW AND IMPROVED

Therefore if anyone is in Christ, he is a new creature; the old things passed away; behold, new things have come.

2 Corinthians 5:17 Holman CSB

Think, for a moment, about the "old" you, the person you were before you invited Christ to reign over your heart. Now, think about the "new" you, the person you have become since then. Is there a difference between the "old" you and the "new and improved" version? There should be! And that difference should be noticeable not only to you but also to others.

The Bible clearly teaches that when we welcome Christ into our hearts, we become new creations through Him. Our challenge, of course, is to behave ourselves like new creations. When we do, God fills our hearts, He blesses our endeavors, and transforms our lives . . . forever.

———

The transforming love of God has repositioned me for eternity. I am now a new man, forgiven, basking in the love of our living God, trusting His promises and provision.

Bill Bright

—Your Thoughts for Today—

ABOVE AND BEYOND
OUR CIRCUMSTANCES

Should we accept only good from God and not adversity?

Job 2:10 Holman CSB

All of us face difficult days. Sometimes even the most devout Christians can become discouraged, and you are no exception. After all, your journey through and beyond cancer is a marathon, and a difficult one, at that.

If you find yourself enduring difficult circumstances, remember that God remains in His heaven. If you become discouraged with the direction of your day, your diagnosis, or your life, turn your thoughts and prayers to Him. He is a God of possibility, not negativity. He will guide you through your difficulties and beyond them . . . far beyond.

Crisis brings us face to face with our inadequacy and our inadequacy in turn leads us to the inexhaustible sufficiency of God.

Catherine Marshall

—Your Thoughts for Today—

STILL LEARNING

Happy is the person who finds wisdom and gains understanding.

Proverbs 3:13 NLT

Spiritual maturity takes time. You simply cannot gain the perspective and insights you need by reading a book, or by listening to a sermon, or by attending a weekend seminar. Of course, you will experience those "aha moments" when you gain a rush of insight. But even then, you will not become instantly mature. The real core of wisdom comes not just from understanding life's most important principles, but also from living in accordance with those principles for years.

So if you're not quite as mature as you'd like to be, don't be discouraged. There are no instantaneous saints. But there are plenty of people (like you) who are slowly becoming more saintly day by day.

If all struggles and sufferings were eliminated, the spirit would no more reach maturity than would the child.

Elisabeth Elliot

—Your Thoughts for Today—

_____

_____

_____

_____

_____

_____

LESSONS TO LEARN

No discipline seems pleasant at the time, but painful. Later on, however, it produces a harvest of righteousness and peace for those who have been trained by it.

Hebrews 12:11 NIV

Whether you're twenty-two or a hundred and two, you've still got lots to learn. God isn't finished with you yet, and He isn't finished teaching you important lessons about life here on earth and life eternal.

God does not intend for you to remain stuck in one place. God wants you to continue growing as a person and as a Christian every day that you live. And make no mistake: both spiritual and intellectual growth are possible during every stage of life—during the happiest days or the hardest ones.

This hard place in which you perhaps find yourself is the very place in which God is giving you opportunity to look only to Him, to spend time in prayer, and to learn long-suffering, gentleness, meekness—in short, to learn the depths of the love that Christ Himself has poured out on all of us.

Elisabeth Elliot

—Your Thoughts for Today—

_____

_____

_____

_____

TO JUDGE OR NOT TO JUDGE

When they persisted in questioning Him, He stood up and said to them, "The one without sin among you should be the first to throw a stone at her."

John 8:7 Holman CSB

A s Jesus came upon a young woman who had been condemned by the Pharisees, He told the people gathered there that only the person who was without sin should cast the first stone. Christ's message applied not only to the Pharisees of ancient times, but also to us. If we genuinely want to experience God's abundance and His joy, we must leave the judging to Him.

So, if you'd like to experience a more peaceful life and a less stressful journey back to health, here's an important step you should take: Refrain from the temptation of judging others. Don't gossip, don't denigrate, don't belittle, and don't malign. Instead, spend your time sharing God's love and spreading His message. It's the peaceful way to live and the best way to heal.

Christians think they are prosecuting attorneys or judges, when, in reality, God has called all of us to be witnesses.

Warren Wiersbe

—Your Thoughts for Today—

ON BEING AN OPTIMISTIC CHRISTIAN

Make me hear joy and gladness.

Psalm 51:8 NKJV

To be a pessimistic Christian is a contradiction in terms, yet sometimes even the most devout Christians fall prey to fear, doubt, and discouragement. But, God has a different plan for our lives. The comforting words of the 23rd Psalm remind us of God's blessings. In response to His grace, we should strive to focus our thoughts on things that are pleasing to Him, not upon things that are evil, discouraging, or frustrating.

So, the next time you find yourself mired in the pit of pessimism, remember God's Word and redirect your thoughts. This world is God's creation; look for the best in it, and trust Him to take care of the rest.

Keep your feet on the ground, but let your heart soar as high as it will. Refuse to be average or to surrender to the chill of your spiritual environment.

A. W. Tozer

—Your Thoughts for Today—

_____

_____

_____

_____

_____

PEACE FOR TODAY

And let the peace of the Messiah, to which you were also called in one body, control your hearts. Be thankful.

Colossians 3:15 Holman CSB

We are imperfect human beings who possess imperfect faith. So it's not surprising that we lose hope from time to time. When we do, we need the encouragement of friends and the life-changing power of prayer.

If we find ourselves falling into the spiritual traps of discouragement, or despair, we should seek guidance from God, and we should solicit support from our family members and friends.

God has promised that peace, joy, and contentment are ours to claim . . . and we should take whatever steps are necessary to claim these gifts. When we guard ourselves against the spiritual snares that might entrap us—emotional traps like worry, discouragement, or fear—we are then free to claim the peace, the contentment, and the power that can—and should—be ours.

Jesus gives us the ultimate rest, the confidence we need, to escape the frustration and chaos of the world around us.

Billy Graham

—Your Thoughts for Today—

_____

_____

_____

WORSHIP HIM ALWAYS

I rejoiced with those who said to me, "Let us go to the house of the Lord."

Psalm 122:1 Holman CSB

All of mankind is engaged in the practice of worship. Some choose to worship God and, as a result, reap the joy that He intends for His children. Others distance themselves from God by worshiping such things as earthly possessions or personal gratification…and when they do so, they suffer.

When we worship God, either alone or in the company of fellow believers, we are blessed. When we fail to worship God, for whatever reason, we forfeit the spiritual riches that are rightfully ours. Every day provides opportunities to put God where He belongs: at the center of our lives. Let us worship Him, and only Him, today and always.

Spiritual worship is focusing all we are on all He is.

Beth Moore

—Your Thoughts for Today—

SEEKING AND FINDING

Ask, and God will give to you. Search, and you will find. Knock, and the door will open for you. Yes, everyone who asks will receive. Everyone who searches will find. And everyone who knocks will have the door opened.

Matthew 7:7-8 NCV

Where is God? He is everywhere you have ever been and everywhere you will ever go. He is with you night and day; He knows your every thought; He hears your every heartbeat.

Sometimes, in the crush of your daily duties, God may seem far away. Or sometimes, when the disappointments and sorrows of life leave you brokenhearted, God may seem distant, but He is not. When you earnestly seek God, you will find Him because He is here, waiting patiently for you to reach out to Him . . . right here . . . right now.

Mark it down. God never turns away the honest seeker. Go to God with your questions. You may not find all the answers, but in finding God, you know the One who does.

Max Lucado

—Your Thoughts for Today—

THE WISDOM TO CELEBRATE

A miserable heart means a miserable life; a cheerful heart fills the day with a song.

Proverbs 15:15 MSG

The Christian life is a cause for celebration, but sometimes we don't feel much like celebrating. In fact, when the weight of the world seems to bear down upon our shoulders, celebration may be the last thing on our minds . . . but it shouldn't be. As God's children, we are all blessed beyond measure on good days and bad. This day is a non-renewable resource— once it's gone, it's gone forever. We should give thanks for this day while using it for the glory of God.

God created you in His own image, and He wants you to experience joy and abundance. But, God will not force His joy upon you; you must claim it for yourself. And that's precisely what you should do.

I may not be able to change the world I see around me, but I can change the way I see the world within me.

John Maxwell

—Your Thoughts for Today—

_____

_____

_____

_____

_____

_____

A PROMISE TO COUNT ON

Blessed is a man who endures trials, because when he passes the test he will receive the crown of life that He has promised to those who love Him.

James 1:12 Holman CSB

Throughout the seasons of life, we must all endure life-altering personal losses that leave us breathless. When we do, we may be overwhelmed by fear, by doubt, or by both. Thankfully, God has promised that He will never desert us. And God keeps His promises.

Life is often challenging, but as Christians, we must trust the promises of our Heavenly Father. God loves us, and He will protect us. In times of hardship, He will comfort us; in times of sorrow, He will dry our tears. When we are troubled, or weak, or sorrowful, God is with us. His love endures, not only for today, but also for all of eternity.

God helps those who help themselves, but there are times when we are quite incapable of helping ourselves. That's when God stoops down and gathers us in His arms like a mother lifts a sick child, and does for us what we cannot do for ourselves.

Ruth Bell Graham

—Your Thoughts for Today—

ACCEPTING HIS GIFTS

What father among you, if his son asks for a fish, will, instead of a fish, give him a snake? Or if he asks for an egg, will give him a scorpion? If you then, who are evil, know how to give good gifts to your children, how much more will the Heavenly Father give the Holy Spirit to those who ask Him?

Luke 11:11-13 Holman CSB

God gives the gifts; we, as believers, should accept them—but oftentimes, we don't. Why? Because we fail to trust our Heavenly Father completely, and because we are, at times, surprisingly stubborn. Luke 11 teaches us that God does not withhold spiritual gifts from those who ask. Our obligation, quite simply, is to ask for them.

Are you asking God to move mountains in your life, or are you expecting Him to stumble over molehills? Whatever the size of your challenges, God is big enough to handle them. Ask for His help today, with faith and with fervor, and then watch in amazement as your mountains begin to move.

The impossible is exactly what God does.

Oswald Chambers

—Your Thoughts for Today—

THE MORNING WATCH

He awakens [Me] each morning; He awakens My ear to listen like those being instructed. The Lord God has opened My ear, and I was not rebellious; I did not turn back.

Isaiah 50:4-5 Holman CSB

Each new day is a gift from God, and if you are wise, you will spend a few quiet moments each morning thanking the Giver.

Warren Wiersbe writes, "Surrender your mind to the Lord at the beginning of each day." And that's sound advice. When you begin each day with your head bowed and your heart lifted, you are reminded of God's love, His protection, and His commandments. Then, you can align your priorities for the coming day with the teachings and commandments that God has placed upon your heart.

So, if you've acquired the unfortunate habit of trying to "squeeze" God into the corners of your life, it's time to reshuffle the items on your to-do list by placing God first. And if you haven't already done so, form the habit of spending quality time with your Father in heaven. He deserves it . . . and so do you.

Meditating upon His Word will inevitably bring peace of mind, strength of purpose, and power for living.

Bill Bright

—Your Thoughts for Today—

DURING DARK DAYS

I have heard your prayer, I have seen your tears; surely I will heal you.

2 Kings 20:5 NKJV

The sadness that accompanies any significant loss is an inevitable fact of life. In time, sadness runs its course and gradually abates. Depression, on the other hand, is a physical and emotional condition that is highly treatable.

If you find yourself feeling "blue," perhaps it's a logical reaction to the ups and downs of daily life. But if you or someone close to you have become dangerously depressed, it's time to seek professional help.

Some days are light and happy, and some days are not. When we face the inevitable dark days of life, we must choose how we will respond. Will we allow ourselves to sink even more deeply into our own sadness, or will we do the difficult work of pulling ourselves out? We bring light to the dark days of life by turning first to God, and then to trusted family members, friends, and medical professionals. When we do, the clouds will eventually part, and the sun will shine once more upon our souls.

—Your Thoughts for Today—

DOING WHAT'S RIGHT

This is how we are sure that we have come to know Him: by keeping His commands.

1 John 2:3 Holman CSB

When we seek righteousness in our own lives—and when we seek the companionship of those who do likewise—we reap the spiritual rewards that God intends for us to enjoy. When we behave ourselves as godly men and women, we honor God. When we live righteously and according to God's commandments, He blesses us in ways that we cannot fully understand.

Today, as you fulfill your responsibilities, hold fast to that which is good, and associate yourself with believers who behave themselves in like fashion. When you do, your good works will serve as a powerful example for others and as a worthy offering to your Creator.

Every time you refuse to face up to life and its problems, you weaken your character.

E. Stanley Jones

—Your Thoughts for Today—

_____

_____

_____

_____

_____

OUR ULTIMATE SAVIOR

And we have seen and testify that the Father has sent the Son as Savior of the world.

1 John 4:14 NKJV

Thomas Brooks spoke for believers of every generation when he observed, "Christ is the sun, and all the watches of our lives should be set by the dial of his motion." Christ, indeed, is the ultimate Savior of mankind and the personal Savior of those who believe in Him. As His servants, we should place Him at the very center of our lives. And, every day that God gives us breath, we should share Christ's love and His message with a world that needs both.

———

There is not a single thing that Jesus cannot change, control, and conquer because He is the living Lord.

Franklin Graham

—Your Thoughts for Today—

_____

_____

_____

_____

_____

_____

_____

_____

THE WORLD . . . AND YOU

Don't copy the behavior and customs of this world, but let God transform you into a new person by changing the way you think.

Romans 12:2 NLT

We live in the world, but we must not worship it. Our duty is to place God first and everything else second. But because we are fallible beings with imperfect faith, placing God in His rightful place is often difficult. In fact, at every turn, or so it seems, we are tempted to do otherwise.

The 21st-century world is a noisy, distracting place filled with countless opportunities to stray from God's will. The world seems to cry, "Worship me with your time, your money, your energy, and your thoughts!" But God commands otherwise: He commands us to worship Him and Him alone; everything else must be secondary.

Christians don't fail to live as they should because they are in the world; they fail because the world has gotten into them.

Billy Graham

—Your Thoughts for Today—

_____

_____

_____

_____

THE SON OF ENCOURAGEMENT

Bright eyes cheer the heart; good news strengthens the bones.
                                                    Proverbs 15:30 Holman CSB

Barnabas, a man whose name meant "Son of Encouragement," was a leader in the early Christian church. He was known for his kindness and for his ability to encourage others. Because of Barnabas, many people were introduced to Christ. And today, as believers living in a difficult world, we must seek to imitate the "Son of Encouragement."

We imitate Barnabas when we speak kind words to our families and to our friends. We imitate Barnabas when our actions give credence to our beliefs. We imitate Barnabas when we are generous with our possessions and with our praise. We imitate Barnabas when we give hope to the hopeless and encouragement to the downtrodden.

Today, be like Barnabas: become a source of encouragement to those who cross your path. When you do so, you will quite literally change the world, one person—and one moment—at a time.

God is still in the process of dispensing gifts, and He uses ordinary individuals like us to develop those gifts in other people.

                                                    Howard Hendricks

—Your Thoughts for Today—

_____

_____

_____

REAL SUCCESS

A new commandment I give to you, that you love one another; as I have loved you, that you also love one another.
John 13:34 NKJV

How do you define success? If you have accepted Christ as your personal Savior, you are already a towering success in the eyes of God, but there is still more that you can do. Your task—as a believer who has been touched by the Creator's grace—is to accept the spiritual abundance and peace that He offers through the person of His Son. Then, when you've discovered God's peace, you are better prepared to share the healing message of His love. When you share God's love with the world, you have indeed reached the pinnacle of success.

The truth of the Gospel is intended to free us to love God and others with our whole heart.

John Eldredge

—Your Thoughts for Today—

_____

_____

_____

_____

_____

_____

_____

STANDING UP
FOR YOUR FAITH

Watch, stand fast in the faith, be brave, be strong.

1 Corinthians 16:13 NKJV

A re you a person whose faith is obvious to your family, to fellow patients, and to the world? God needs more men and women who are willing to stand up and be counted for Him.

Genuine faith is never meant to be locked up in the heart of a believer; to the contrary, it is meant to be shared. And believers who wish to share God's Good News with the world should begin by sharing that message with their own family.

Through every triumph and tragedy, God will stand by your side and strengthen you . . . if you have faith in Him. Jesus taught His disciples that if they had faith, they could move mountains. You can too, and so can your family . . . if you have faith.

Trials are not enemies of faith but opportunities to reveal God's faithfulness.

Barbara Johnson

In my weakness, I have learned, like Moses, to lean hard on God. The weaker I am, the harder I lean on Him. The harder I lean, the stronger I discover Him to be. The stronger I discover God to be, the more resolute I am in this job He's given me to do.

Joni Eareckson Tada

God takes us through struggles and difficulties so that we might become increasingly committed to Him.

Charles Swindoll

Our faith grows by expression. If we want to keep our faith, we must share it. We must act.

Billy Graham

Hope must be in the future tense. Faith, to be faith, must always be in the present tense.

Catherine Marshall

—Your Thoughts for Today—

THE WISDOM TO OBEY

If you love Me, you will keep My commandments.

John 14:15 Holman CSB

Since God created Adam and Eve, we human beings have been rebelling against our Creator. Why? Because we are unwilling to trust God's Word, and we are unwilling to follow His commandments. God has given us a guidebook for righteous living called the Holy Bible. It contains thorough instructions which, if followed, lead to fulfillment, righteousness and salvation. But, if we choose to disregard God's commandments, the results are as predictable as they are unfortunate.

Talking about God is easy; living by His commandments is considerably harder. But, unless we are willing to abide by God's laws, all of our righteous proclamations ring hollow. How can we best proclaim our love for the Lord? By obeying Him. And, for further instructions, read the manual.

God will never reveal more truth about Himself until you have obeyed what you know already.

Oswald Chambers

—Your Thoughts for Today—

_____

_____

_____

_____

_____

NOW IS THE TIME

So, my son, throw yourself into this work for Christ.

2 Timothy 1:1 MSG

God's love for you is deeper and more profound than you can imagine. God's love for you is so great that He sent His only Son to this earth to die for your sins and to offer you the priceless gift of eternal life. Now, you must decide whether or not to accept God's gift.

Your decision to allow Christ to reign over your heart is the pivotal decision of your life. It is a decision that you cannot ignore. It is a decision that is yours and yours alone. Accept God's gift now: allow His Son to preside over your heart, your thoughts, and your life, starting this very instant.

Among the most joyful people I have known have been some who seem to have had no human reason for joy. The sweet fragrance of Christ has shown through their lives.

Elisabeth Elliot

—Your Thoughts for Today—

A LIFE OF FULFILLMENT

For You, O God, have tested us; You have refined us as silver is refined . . . we went through fire and through water; but You brought us out to rich fulfillment.

Psalm 66:10–12 NKJV

Everywhere we turn, or so it seems, the world promises fulfillment, contentment, and happiness. But the contentment that the world offers is fleeting and incomplete. Thankfully, the fulfillment that God offers is all encompassing and everlasting.

Sometimes, on the journey through illness and beyond, we can forfeit—albeit temporarily—the joy of Christ as we wrestle with the challenges of daily living. Yet God's Word is clear: fulfillment through Christ is available to all who seek it and claim it. Count yourself among that number. Seek first a personal, transforming relationship with Jesus, and then claim the joy, the fulfillment, and the spiritual abundance that the Shepherd offers His sheep.

We are never more fulfilled than when our longing for God is met by His presence in our lives.

Billy Graham

—Your Thoughts for Today—

GOD IS LOVE

God is love; and he that dwelleth in love dwelleth in God, and God in him.

1 John 4:16 KJV

The Bible makes this promise: God is love. It's a sweeping statement, a profoundly important description of what God is and how God works. God's love is perfect. When we open our hearts to His perfect love, we are touched by the Creator's hand, and we are transformed.

Today, even if you can only carve out a few quiet moments, offer sincere prayers of thanksgiving to your Creator. He loves you now and throughout all eternity. Open your heart to His presence and His love.

———

Even when we cannot see the why and wherefore of God's dealings, we know that there is love in and behind them, so we can rejoice always.

J. I. Packer

—Your Thoughts for Today—

WHY HE SENT HIS SON

For all have sinned and fall short of the glory of God.

Romans 3:23 Holman CSB

Despite our shortcomings, God sent His Son so that we might be redeemed from our sins. In doing so, our Heavenly Father demonstrated His infinite mercy and His infinite love. We have received countless gifts from God, but none can compare with the gift of salvation. God's grace is the ultimate gift, and we owe Him the ultimate in thanksgiving.

Christ sacrificed His life on the cross so that we might have eternal life. This gift, freely given from God's only begotten Son, is the priceless possession of everyone who accepts Him as Lord and Savior. We return our Savior's love by welcoming Him into our hearts and sharing His message and His love. When we do so, we are blessed here on earth and throughout all eternity.

The grace of God is the one thing we cannot do without in this life or in the life to come; it has no substitutes, artificial, temporary, or otherwise.

Bill Bright

—Your Thoughts for Today—

_____

_____

_____

_____

_____

A WORTHY DISCIPLE

He has told you men what is good and what it is the Lord requires of you: Only to act justly, to love faithfulness, and to walk humbly with your God.

Micah 6:8 Holman CSB

When Jesus addressed His disciples, He warned that each one must, "take up his cross and follow me." The disciples must have known exactly what the Master meant. In Jesus' day, prisoners were forced to carry their own crosses to the location where they would be put to death. Thus, Christ's message was clear: in order to follow Him, Christ's disciples must deny themselves and, instead, trust Him completely. Nothing has changed since then.

If we are to be disciples of Christ, we must trust Him and place Him at the very center of our beings. Jesus never comes "next." He is always first.

Do you seek to be a worthy disciple of Christ? Then pick up His cross today and every day that you live. When you do, He will bless you now and forever.

Discipleship is a daily discipline: we follow Jesus a step at a time, a day at a time.

Warren Wiersbe

—Your Thoughts for Today—

SHOUTING THE GOOD NEWS

As you go, announce this: "The kingdom of heaven has come near."

Matthew 10:7 Holman CSB

The Good News of Jesus Christ should be shouted from the rooftops by believers the world over. But all too often, it is not. For a variety of reasons, many Christians keep their beliefs to themselves, and when they do, the world suffers because of their failure to speak up.

As believers, we are called to share the transforming message of Jesus with our families, with our neighbors, and with the world. Jesus commands us to become fishers of men. And, the time to go fishing is now. We must share the Good News of Jesus Christ today—tomorrow may indeed be too late.

The evangelistic harvest is always urgent. The destiny of men and of nations is always being decided. God will hold us responsible as to how well we fulfill our responsibilities and take advantage of our opportunities.

Billy Graham

—Your Thoughts for Today—

LOVE ONE ANOTHER

Beloved, if God so loved us, we also ought to love one another.

1 John 4:11 NKJV

Love, like everything else in this wonderful world, begins and ends with God, but the middle part belongs to us. During the brief time that we have here on earth, God has given each of us the opportunity to become a loving person—or not. God has given each of us the opportunity to be kind, to be courteous, to be cooperative, and to be forgiving—or not.

God has given each of us the chance to obey the Golden Rule, or to make up our own rules as we go. If we obey God's rules, we're safe, but if we do otherwise, we're headed for trouble and fast.

Here in the real world, the choices that we make have consequences. The decisions that we make and the results of those decisions determine the quality of our relationships. It's as simple as that.

How do you spell love? True love is spelled G-I-V-E.

Josh McDowell

—Your Thoughts for Today—

_____

_____

_____

_____

_____

PATIENCE PAYS

Knowing God leads to self-control. Self-control leads to patient endurance, and patient endurance leads to godliness.
2 Peter 1:6 NLT

Being patient with other people can be difficult. But sometimes we find it even more difficult to be patient with ourselves. When we're ill, we want healing now, not later. And we want our lives to unfold according to our own timetables. But what about God's timetable? Obviously, God's timetable supersedes our own, whether we like it or not.

The Bible clearly instructs us that patience and wisdom are traveling companions. For most of us, learning the art of patience means learning to accept our circumstances, our family members, our doctors, and ourselves. When we learn patience, God smiles . . . and so do our friends and neighbors.

The next time you're disappointed, don't panic and don't give up. Just be patient and let God remind you he's still in control.

Max Lucado

—Your Thoughts for Today—

_____

_____

_____

_____

_____

BE STEADFAST

We also rejoice in our afflictions, because we know that affliction produces endurance, endurance produces proven character, and proven character produces hope.

Romans 5:3-4 Holman CSB

In a world filled with roadblocks and stumbling blocks, we need strength, courage, and perseverance. And, as an example of perfect perseverance, we need look no further than our Savior, Jesus Christ.

Jesus finished what He began, and so must we.

Perhaps you are in a hurry for God to restore your confidence and your health. If so, be forewarned: God operates on His own timetable, not yours. Sometimes, God may answer your prayers with silence, and when He does, you must patiently persevere. In times of trouble, you must remain steadfast and trust in the merciful goodness of your Heavenly Father. Whatever your problem, He can fix it. Your job is to keep praying—and working—until He does.

No matter how heavy the burden, daily strength is given, so I expect we need not give ourselves any concern as to what the outcome will be. We must simply go forward.

Annie Armstrong

—Your Thoughts for Today—

ENTHUSIASTIC SERVICE

Do your work with enthusiasm. Work as if you were serving the Lord, not as if you were serving only men and women.

Ephesians 6:7 NCV

Despite your illness, do you see each day as a glorious opportunity to serve God and to do His will? Are you enthused about life, or do you struggle through each day giving scarcely a thought to God's blessings? Are you constantly praising God for His gifts, and are you sharing His Good News with the world? And, are you excited about the possibilities for service that God has placed before you? You should be.

You are the recipient of Christ's sacrificial love. Accept it enthusiastically and share it fervently. Jesus deserves your enthusiasm; the world deserves it; and you deserve the experience of sharing it.

One of the great needs in the church today is for every Christian to become enthusiastic about his faith in Jesus Christ.

Billy Graham

—Your Thoughts for Today—

ABUNDANT PEACE

The peace of God, which surpasses all understanding, will guard your hearts and minds through Christ Jesus.
Philippians 4:7 NKJV

In every season of life, in good times and hard times, God offers abundance. If you are a thoughtful believer, you will open yourself to the spiritual abundance that your Savior offers by following Him completely and without reservation. When you do, you will receive the love, the peace, and the joy that He has promised.

Do you sincerely seek the riches that our Savior offers to those who give themselves to Him? Then follow Him today and every day. Seek first the salvation that is available through a personal, passionate relationship with Christ, and then claim the joy, the peace, and the spiritual abundance that the Shepherd offers His sheep.

Instead of living a black-and-white existence, we'll be released into a Technicolor world of vibrancy and emotion when we more accurately reflect His nature to the world around us.

Bill Hybels

—Your Thoughts for Today—

_____

_____

_____

_____

_____

BEYOND ANXIETY

In the multitude of my anxieties within me, Your comforts delight my soul.

Psalm 94:19 NKJV

God calls us to live above and beyond anxiety. God calls us to live by faith, not by fear. He instructs us to trust Him completely, this day and forever. But sometimes, trusting God is difficult, especially when we become caught up in the incessant demands of an anxious world.

When you feel anxious—and you will—return your thoughts to God's love. Then, take your concerns to Him in prayer, and to the best of your ability, leave them there. Whatever "it" is, God is big enough to handle it. Let Him. Now.

Worry and anxiety are sand in the machinery of life; faith is the oil.

E. Stanley Jones

—Your Thoughts for Today—

CONTAGIOUS CHRISTIANITY

This good news of the kingdom will be proclaimed in all the world as a testimony to all nations.

Matthew 24:14 Holman CSB

Genuine, heartfelt Christianity can be highly contagious. When you've experienced the transforming power of God's love, you feel the need to share the Good News of His only begotten Son. So, whether you realize it or not, you can be sure that you are being led to share the story of your faith with family, with friends, and with the world.

Every believer, including you, bears responsibility for sharing God's Good News. And it is important to remember that you share your testimony through words and actions, but not necessarily in that order.

Today, don't be bashful or timid: Talk about Jesus and, while you're at it, show the world what it really means to follow Him. After all, the fields are ripe for the harvest, time is short, and the workers are surprisingly few. So please share your story today because tomorrow may indeed be too late.

———

Nothing else you do will ever matter as much as helping people establish an eternal relationship with God!

Rick Warren

—Your Thoughts for Today—

SPIRITUAL SICKNESS

Don't insist on getting even; that's not for you to do. "I'll do the judging," says God. "I'll take care of it."

Romans 12:19 MSG

Bitterness is a spiritual sickness. It will consume your soul; it is dangerous to your emotional health. It can destroy you if you let it . . . so don't let it!

If you are caught up in intense feelings of anger or resentment, you know all too well the destructive power of these emotions. How can you rid yourself of these feelings? First, you must prayerfully ask God to cleanse your heart. Then, you must learn to catch yourself whenever thoughts of bitterness or hatred begin to attack you. Your challenge is this: You must learn to resist negative thoughts before they hijack your emotions.

Bitterness is the trap that snares the hunter.

Max Lucado

—Your Thoughts for Today—

FINDING ENCOURAGEMENT

Haven't I commanded you: be strong and courageous? Do not be afraid or discouraged, for the Lord your God is with you wherever you go.

Joshua 1:9 Holman CSB

God offers us the strength to meet our challenges, and He offers us hope for the future. One way that He shares His message of hope is through the words of encouraging friends and family members.

Hope, like other human emotions, is contagious. If we associate with hope-filled, enthusiastic people, their enthusiasm will have a tendency to lift our spirits. But if we find ourselves spending too much time in the company of naysayers, pessimists, or cynics, our thoughts—like the naysayers'—will tend to be negative.

Are you a hopeful, optimistic Christian? And do you associate with like-minded people? If so, then you're both wise and blessed.

What is the cure for disillusionment? Putting our complete hope and trust in the living Lord.

Charles Swindoll

—Your Thoughts for Today—

_____

_____

_____

_____

_____

BEYOND YOUR DOUBTS

Immediately the father of the boy cried out, "I do believe! Help my unbelief."

Mark 9:24 Holman CSB

Doubts come in several shapes and sizes: doubts about God, doubts about the future, and doubts about our own abilities, for starters. But when doubts creep in, as they will from time to time, we need not despair. As Sheila Walsh observed, "To wrestle with God does not mean that we have lost faith, but that we are fighting for it."

Whenever you're plagued by doubts, that's precisely the moment you should seek God's presence by genuinely seeking to establish a deeper, more meaningful relationship with His Son. Then you may rest assured that in time, God will calm your fears, answer your prayers, and restore your confidence.

Struggling with God over the issues of life doesn't show a lack of faith—that is faith.

Lee Strobel

—Your Thoughts for Today—

THE GREATEST AMONG US

The greatest among you will be your servant. Whoever exalts himself will be humbled, and whoever humbles himself will be exalted.

Matthew 23:11-12 Holman CSB

J esus teaches that the most esteemed men and women are not the leaders of society or the captains of industry. To the contrary, Jesus teaches that the greatest among us are those who choose to minister and to serve.

Today, you will have many opportunities to serve. Serve quietly and without fanfare. Then, when you have done your best to help family, friends, and fellow patients, you can rest comfortably knowing that in the eyes of God you have achieved greatness. And God's eyes, after all, are the only ones that really count.

God will open up places of service for you as He sees you are ready. Meanwhile, study the Bible and give yourself a chance to grow.

Warren Wiersbe

—Your Thoughts for Today—

_____

_____

_____

_____

_____

_____

_____

GOD AND FAMILY

Let the Word of Christ—the Message—have the run of the house. Give it plenty of room in your lives.

Colossians 3:16 MSG

These may be difficult days for you and your family. But, thankfully, God is bigger than any challenge you face.

God loves us and protects us. In times of trouble, He comforts us; in times of sorrow, He dries our tears. When we are troubled, or weak, or sorrowful, God is as near as our next breath.

We live in a world where temptation, danger, and discouragement seem to lurk on every street corner. Parents and children alike have good reason to be watchful. But, despite the dangers of our time, God remains steadfast. Even in these difficult days, no problem is too big for God.

Apart from religious influence, the family is the most important influence on society.

Billy Graham

—Your Thoughts for Today—

_____

_____

_____

_____

_____

THE LAST WORD

For God has not given us a spirit of fearfulness, but one of power, love, and sound judgment. So don't be ashamed of the testimony about our Lord, or of me His prisoner. Instead, share in suffering for the gospel, relying on the power of God.
2 Timothy 1:7-8 Holman CSB

All of us may find our courage tested by the inevitable disappointments and tragedies of life. After all, ours is a world filled with uncertainty, hardship, sickness, and danger. Old Man Trouble, it seems, is never too far from the front door.

When we focus upon our fears and our doubts, we may find many reasons to lie awake at night and fret about the uncertainties of the coming day. A better strategy, of course, is to focus not upon our fears, but instead upon our God.

God is your shield and your strength; you are His forever. So don't focus your thoughts upon the fears of the day. Instead, trust God's plan and His eternal love for you. And remember: God is good, and He has the last word.

———

Fear is a self-imposed prison that will keep you from becoming what God intends for you to be.

Rick Warren

—Your Thoughts for Today—

_____

_____

_____

FORGIVE: IT'S GOD'S WAY

And be kind and compassionate to one another, forgiving one another, just as God also forgave you in Christ.

Ephesians 4:32 Holman CSB

To forgive others is difficult. Being frail, fallible, imperfect human beings, we are quick to anger, quick to blame, slow to forgive, and even slower to forget. No matter. Forgiveness, no matter how difficult, is God's way, and it must be our way, too.

God's commandments are not intended to be customized for the particular whims of particular believers. God's Word is not a menu from which each of us may select items à la carte, according to our own desires. Far from it. God's Holy Word is a book that must be taken in its entirety; all of God's commandments are to be taken seriously. And, so it is with forgiveness. So, if you hold bitterness against even a single person, forgive. Then, to the best of your abilities, forget. It's God's way for you to live.

———

As you forgive others, winter will soon make way for springtime as fresh joy pushes up through the soil of your heart.

Barbara Johnson

—Your Thoughts for Today—

_____

_____

_____

_____

BEYOND THE PAIN

I called to the Lord in my distress; I called to my God. From His temple He heard my voice.

2 Samuel 22:7 Holman CSB

The pain of any significant illness can be intense, and so it is with cancer. Thankfully, God's promises give us hope: some day, perhaps some day soon, the pain will diminish.

Barbara Johnson writes, "There is no way around suffering. We have to go through it to get to the other side." The best way "to get to the other side" of suffering is to get there with God. When we turn open hearts to Him in heartfelt prayer, He will answer in His own way and in His own time. And while we're waiting for His answer, we can be certain that we will be protected by Him, now and forever.

Pain is inevitable, but misery is optional.

Max Lucado

—Your Thoughts for Today—

_____

_____

_____

_____

_____

_____

HEEDING GOD'S CALL

One thing I do, forgetting those things which are behind and reaching forward to those things which are ahead, I press toward the goal for the prize of the upward call of God in Christ Jesus.

Philippians 3:13-14 NKJV

As you journey through and beyond your illness, it is vitally important that you continue to heed God's call. In John 15:16, Jesus says, "You did not choose me, but I chose you and appointed you to go and bear fruit—fruit that will last" (NIV). In other words, you have been called by Christ at this very moment, at the very place where you happen to be. Now, it is up to you to decide precisely how you will answer. And as you're thinking about your answer, remember this: God has important work for you to do—work that no one else on earth can accomplish but you.

When you become consumed by God's call on your life, everything will take on new meaning and significance. You will begin to see every facet of your life, including your pain, as a means through which God can bring others to Himself.

Charles Stanley

—Your Thoughts for Today—

TRUST HIM TO GUIDE YOU

The fear of man is a snare, but the one who trusts in the Lord is protected.

Proverbs 29:25 Holman CSB

A s Christians whose salvation has been purchased by the blood of Christ, we have every reason to live joyously and courageously. After all, Christ has already fought and won our battle for us— He did so on the cross at Calvary. But despite Christ's sacrifice, and despite God's promises, we may become confused or disoriented by the endless complications and countless distractions of modern living.

If you're unsure of your next step, lean upon God's promises and lift your prayers to Him. Remember that God is your protector. Open yourself to His heart, and trust Him to guide you. When you do, God will direct your steps, and you will receive His blessings today, tomorrow, and throughout eternity.

We must always invite Jesus to be the navigator of our plans, desires, wills, and emotions, for He is the way, the truth, and the life.

Bill Bright

—Your Thoughts for Today—

ULTIMATE PROTECTION

The Lord is the One who will go before you. He will be with you; He will not leave you or forsake you. Do not be afraid or discouraged.

Deuteronomy 31:8 Holman CSB

God has promised to protect us, and He intends to fulfill His promise. In a world filled with dangers and temptations, God is the ultimate armor. In a world filled with misleading messages, God's Word is the ultimate truth. In a world filled with more frustrations than we can count, God's Son offers the ultimate peace.

Will you accept God's peace and wear God's armor against the dangers of our world? Hopefully so, because when you do, you can live courageously, knowing that you possess the ultimate protection: God's unfailing love for you.

The promises of God's Word sustain us in our suffering, and we know Jesus sympathizes and empathizes with us in our darkest hour.

Bill Bright

—Your Thoughts for Today—

_____

_____

_____

_____

_____

HOW TO TREAT OTHERS:
A SIMPLE RULE OF THUMB

Therefore, whatever you want others to do for you, do also the same for them—this is the Law and the Prophets?

Matthew 7:12 Holman CSB

As Christians, we are instructed to be courteous and compassionate. As believers, we are called to be gracious, humble, gentle, and kind. But sometimes, we fall short. Sometimes, amid the busyness and distractions of everyday life, we may neglect to share a kind word or a kind deed. This oversight hurts others, and it hurts us as well.

Today, even if you're weary, or hurting, or both, slow yourself down and be alert for those who need your smile, your kind words, or your helping hand. Make kindness a centerpiece of your dealings with others. They will be blessed, and you will be, too. So make this promise to yourself and keep it: honor Christ by obeying His Golden Rule. He deserves no less. And neither, for that matter, do they.

When you launch an act of kindness out into the crosswinds of life, it will blow kindness back to you.

Dennis Swanberg

—Your Thoughts for Today—

_____

_____

_____

_____

YOUR TRUE HOME

In My Father's house are many dwelling places; if not, I would have told you. I am going away to prepare a place for you. If I go away and prepare a place for you, I will come back and receive you to Myself, so that where I am you may be also.

John 14:2-3 Holman CSB

Our troubles are easier to tolerate when we remind ourselves that heaven is our true home. An old hymn contains the words, "This world is not my home; I'm just passing through." Thank goodness!

This crazy world can be a place of trouble and danger. Thankfully, God has offered you a permanent home in heaven, a place of unimaginable glory, a place that your Heavenly Father has already prepared for you,

Jesus tells us He has prepared a place for us. We should trust Him, and we should obey His commandments. When we do, we can withstand any problem, knowing that our troubles are temporary, but that heaven is not.

—Your Thoughts for Today—

_____

_____

_____

_____

CONDUCT AND CHARACTER

Lead a quiet and peaceable life in all godliness and honesty.
1 Timothy 2:2 KJV

Charles Stanley said, "The Bible teaches that we are accountable to one another for our conduct and character." As believers in Christ, we must seek to live each day with discipline, honesty, and faith. When we do, at least two things happen: integrity becomes a habit, and God blesses us because of our obedience to Him. Living a life of integrity isn't always the easiest way, but it is always the right way, and God clearly intends that it should be our way, too.

As you make the journey through and beyond your illness, you'll need character, and lots of it. When you need strength, look to God and study His Word. When you do, your decisions will be sound, and your character will take care of itself.

The trials of life can be God's tools for engraving His image on our character.

Warren Wiersbe

—Your Thoughts for Today—

_____

_____

_____

_____

_____

_____

READY. SET. GO!

Do not neglect the gift that is in you.

1 Timothy 4:14 Holman CSB

The gifts that you possess are gifts from the Giver of all things good. Do you have a spiritual gift? Share it. Do you have a testimony about the things that Christ has done for you? Don't leave your story untold. Do you possess financial resources? Share them. Do you have particular talents? Hone your skills and use them for God's glory.

When you obey God by sharing His gifts freely and without fanfare, you invite Him to bless you more and more. Today, be a faithful steward of your talents and experiences. And then prepare yourself for even greater blessings that are sure to come.

One thing taught large in the Holy Scriptures is that while God gives His gifts freely, He will require a strict accounting of them at the end of the road.

A. W. Tozer

—Your Thoughts for Today—

GREAT IS THY FAITHFULNESS

God is faithful, by whom you were called into the fellowship of His Son, Jesus Christ our Lord.

1 Corinthians 1:9 NKJV

God is faithful to us even when we are not faithful to Him. God keeps His promises to us even when we stray far from His will. He continues to love us even when we disobey His commandments. But God does not force His blessings upon us. If we are to experience His love and His grace, we must claim them for ourselves.

Are you tired, discouraged or fearful? Be comforted: God is with you. Are you confused? Listen to the quiet voice of your Heavenly Father. Are you bitter? Talk with God and seek His guidance. Are you celebrating a great victory? Thank God and praise Him. He is the Giver of all things good. In whatever condition you find yourself, trust God and be comforted. The Father is with you now and forever.

God's faithfulness has never depended on the faithfulness of his children. God is greater than our weakness. In fact, I think, it is our weakness that reveals how great God is.

Max Lucado

—Your Thoughts for Today—

_____

_____

_____

_____

WAIT FOR THE LORD

I waited patiently for the Lord, and He turned to me and heard my cry for help. He brought me up from a desolate pit, out of the muddy clay, and set my feet on a rock, making my steps secure. He put a new song in my mouth, a hymn of praise to our God.

Psalm 40:1-3 Holman CSB

Are you facing a difficult time in your recovery? Are you tired, or troubled, or both? Are you burdened by sadness or discouragement that seems almost too much to bear? If so, remember the words of Winston Churchill: "Never give in!" And remember this: Whatever the size of your challenge, God is bigger. And He always has the final word.

You cannot persevere unless there is a trial in your life. There can be no victories without battles; there can be no peaks without valleys. If you want the blessing, you must be prepared to carry the burden and fight the battle. God has to balance privileges with responsibilities, blessings with burdens, or else you and I will become spoiled, pampered children.

Warren Wiersbe

Stand still and refuse to retreat. Look at it as God looks at it and draw upon his power to hold up under the blast.

Charles Swindoll

Our loving God uses difficulty in our lives to burn away the sin of self and build faith and spiritual power.

Bill Bright

No matter what trials we face, Christ never leaves us.

Billy Graham

Each problem is a God-appointed instructor.

Charles Swindoll

The roots grow deep when the winds are strong.

Charles Swindoll

—Your Thoughts for Today—

_____

_____

_____

_____

_____

_____

_____

_____

_____

_____

_____

WITH YOU ALWAYS

You reveal the path of life to me; in Your presence is abundant joy; in Your right hand are eternal pleasures.

Psalm 16:11 Holman CSB

Do you ever wonder if God is really here? If so, you're not the first person to think such thoughts. In fact, some of the biggest heroes in the Bible had their doubts—and so, perhaps, will you. But when questions arise and doubts begin to creep into your mind, remember this: You can talk with God any time. In fact, He's right here, right now, listening to your thoughts and prayers, watching over your every move.

Sometimes, you will allow yourself to become very busy, and that's when you may be tempted to ignore God. But, when you quiet yourself long enough to acknowledge His presence, God will touch your heart and restore your spirits. By the way, He's ready to talk right now. Are you?

Remember, we go through nothing that God does not know about.

Oswald Chambers

—Your Thoughts for Today—

CELEBRATING OTHERS

Therefore encourage one another and build each other up as you are already doing.

1 Thessalonians 5:11 Holman CSB

As Christians, we are called upon to spread the Good News of Christ, and we are also called to spread a message of encouragement and hope to the world. Each day provides countless opportunities to encourage others and to praise their victories. When we do so, we not only spread seeds of joy and happiness, but we also obey the commandments of God's Holy Word.

Today, make up your mind to be a cheerful Christian, with a smile on your face and encouraging words on your lips. By blessing others, you will also bless yourself. By encouraging others, you'll give honor to the One who gave His life for you.

You can't light another's path without casting light on your own.

John Maxwell

—Your Thoughts for Today—

_____

_____

_____

_____

_____

_____

COURTESY MATTERS

Out of respect for Christ, be courteously reverent to one another.

Ephesians 5:21 MSG

id Christ instruct us in matters of etiquette and courtesy? Of course He did. Christ's instructions are clear: "In everything, therefore, treat people the same way you want them to treat you, for this is the Law and the Prophets" (Matthew 7:12 NASB). Jesus did not say, "In some things, treat people as you wish to be treated." And, He did not say, "From time to time, treat others with kindness." Christ said that we should treat others as we wish to be treated in every aspect of our daily lives.

Even if you're feeling tired or troubled today, be a little kinder than necessary to family members, friends, fellow patients, and total strangers. As you consider all the things that Christ has done in your life, honor Him with your words and with your deeds. He expects no less, and He deserves no less.

When you extend hospitality to others, you're not trying to impress people; you're trying to reflect God to them.

Max Lucado

—Your Thoughts for Today—

_____

_____

_____

_____

PLACING GOD FIRST

So that at the name of Jesus every knee should bow—of those who are in heaven and on earth and under the earth—and every tongue should confess that Jesus Christ is Lord, to the glory of God the Father.

Philippians 2:10-11 Holman CSB

As you think about the nature of your relationship with God, remember this: you will always have some type of relationship with Him—it is inevitable that your life must be lived in relationship to God. The question is not if you will have a relationship with Him; the burning question is whether that relationship will be one that seeks to honor Him . . . or not.

Are you willing to place God first in your life? And, are you willing to welcome Him into your heart? Unless you can honestly answer these questions with a resounding yes, then your relationship with God isn't what it could be or should be. Thankfully, God is always available, He's always ready to forgive, and He's waiting to hear from you now. The rest, of course, is up to you.

O God. You are always the same. Let me know myself and know You.

St. Augustine

—Your Thoughts for Today—

LESSONS LEARNED AND SHARED

When I was a child, I spoke like a child, I thought like a child, I reasoned like a child. When I became a man, I put aside childish things.

1 Corinthians 13:11 Holman CSB

How can you make sure that you'll keep growing (and learning) during good times and hard times? You do so through prayer, through worship, through fellowship, through an openness to God's Holy Spirit, and through a careful study of God's Holy Word.

Your Bible contains powerful prescriptions for overcoming tough times. When you study God's Word and live according to His commandments, adversity becomes a practical instructor. While you're enduring difficult days, you learn lessons you simply could not have learned any other way. And when you learn those lessons, you will serve as a shining example to your friends, to your family, and to the world.

Growth in depth and strength and consistency and fruitfulness and ultimately in Christlikeness is only possible when the winds of life are contrary to personal comfort.

Anne Graham Lotz

—Your Thoughts for Today—

TRUST THE LORD

The one who understands a matter finds success, and the one who trusts in the Lord will be happy.

Proverbs 16:20 Holman CSB

Where will you place your trust today? Will you trust in the ways of the world, or will you trust in the Word and the will of your Creator?

If you aspire to do great things for God's kingdom, you will trust Him completely.

Trusting God means trusting Him in every aspect of your life. You must trust Him with your relationships. You must trust Him with your finances. You must follow His commandments and pray for His guidance. Then, you can wait patiently for God's revelations and for His blessings.

When you trust your Heavenly Father without reservation, you can rest assured: in His own fashion and in His own time, God will bless you in ways that you never could have imagined. So trust Him, and then prepare yourself for the abundance and joy that will most certainly be yours through Him.

How changed our lives would be if we could only fly through the days on wings of surrender and trust!

Hannah Whitall Smith

—Your Thoughts for Today—

FILLED WITH THE SPIRIT

And don't get drunk with wine, which leads to reckless actions, but be filled with the Spirit.

Ephesians 5:18 Holman CSB

When you are filled with the Holy Spirit, your words and deeds will reflect a love and devotion to Christ. When you are filled with the Holy Spirit, the steps of your life's journey are guided by the Lord. When you allow God's Spirit to work in you and through you, you will be energized and transformed.

Today, allow yourself to be filled with the Spirit of God. And then stand back in amazement as God begins to work miracles in your own life and in the lives of those you love.

The Holy Spirit is like a living and continually flowing fountain in believers. We have the boundless privilege of tapping into that fountain every time we pray.

Shirley Dobson

—Your Thoughts for Today—

HOPE FOR TODAY

You have already heard about this hope in the message of truth, the gospel that has come to you. It is bearing fruit and growing all over the world, just as it has among you since the day you heard it and recognized God's grace in the truth.

Colossians 1:5-6 Holman CSB

Despite God's promises, despite Christ's love, and despite our countless blessings, we frail human beings can still lose hope from time to time. When we do, we need the encouragement of Christian friends, the life-changing power of prayer, and the healing truth of God's Holy Word. If we find ourselves falling into the spiritual traps of worry and discouragement, we should seek the healing touch of Jesus and the encouraging words of fellow Christians. Even though this world can be a place of trials and struggles, God has promised us peace, joy, and eternal life if we give ourselves to Him. And, of course, God keeps His promises today, tomorrow, and forever.

———

Teach us to set our hopes on heaven, to hold firmly to the promise of eternal life, so that we can withstand the struggles and storms of this world.

Max Lucado

—Your Thoughts for Today—

_____

_____

_____

_____

A SHINING LIGHT

While ye have light, believe in the light, that ye may be the children of light.

John 12:36 KJV

The Bible says that you are "the light that gives light to the world." What kind of light have you been giving off? Hopefully, you've been a good example for everybody to see. Why? Because the world needs all the light it can get, and that includes your light, too.

Christ showed enduring love for you by willingly sacrificing His own life so that you might have eternal life. As a response to His sacrifice, you should love Him, praise Him, and share His message of salvation with your neighbors and with the world. So let your light shine today and every day. When you do, God will bless you now and forever.

Whatever clouds you face today, ask Jesus, the light of the world, to help you look behind the cloud to see His glory and His plans for you.

Billy Graham

—Your Thoughts for Today—

TRUSTING HIS MIRACULOUS POWER

Now glory be to God! By his mighty power at work within us, he is able to accomplish infinitely more than we would ever dare to ask or hope.

Ephesians 3:20 NLT

Sometimes, because we are imperfect human beings with limited understanding and limited faith, we place limitations on God. But, God's power has no limitations. God will work miracles in our lives if we trust Him with everything we have and everything we are. When we do, we experience the miraculous results of His endless love and His awesome power.

Do you lack the faith that God can work miracles in your own life? If so, it's time to reconsider. Are you a "Doubting Thomas," or a "Negative Nelly"? If so, you are attempting to place limitations on a God who has none. Instead, you must trust in God and trust in His power. Then, you must wait patiently . . . because something miraculous is just about to happen.

Miracles are not contrary to nature but only contrary to what we know about nature.

St. Augustine

—Your Thoughts for Today—

HIS INTIMATE LOVE

As the Father loved Me, I also have loved you; abide in My love.

John 15:9 NKJV

St. Augustine observed, "God loves each of us as if there were only one of us." Do you believe those words? Do you seek an intimate, one-on-one relationship with your Heavenly Father, or are you satisfied to keep Him at a "safe" distance?

Sometimes, in the crush of our daily duties, God may seem far away, but He is not. God is everywhere we have ever been and everywhere we will ever go. He is with us night and day; He knows our thoughts and our prayers. And, when we earnestly seek Him, we will find Him because He is here, waiting patiently for us to reach out to Him. May we reach out to Him today and always. And may we praise Him for the glorious gifts that have transformed us today and forever.

The love of God is one of the great realities of the universe, a pillar upon which the hope of the world rests. But it is a personal, intimate thing too. God does not love populations. He loves people. He loves not masses, but men.

A. W. Tozer

—Your Thoughts for Today—

SUFFICIENT FOR YOUR NEEDS

And God is able to make all grace abound toward you, that you, always having all sufficiency in all things, may have an abundance for every good work.

2 Corinthians 9:8 NKJV

Of this you can be sure: the love of God is sufficient to meet your needs. Whatever challenges you may face, whatever heartbreaks you must endure, God is with you, and He stands ready to comfort you and heal your heart.

The Psalmist writes, "Weeping may endure for a night, but joy comes in the morning" (Psalm 30:5 NKJV). But when we are suffering, the morning may seem very far away. It is not. God promises that He is "near to those who have a broken heart" (Psalm 34:18 NKJV).

If you are experiencing tough times, remember that this day, like every other, is simply another stage of your journey with God. And, be mindful of this fact: the loving heart of God is sufficient to meet any challenge, including yours.

———

The grace of God is sufficient for all our needs, for every problem and for every difficulty, for every broken heart, and for every human sorrow.

Peter Marshall

—Your Thoughts for Today—

_____

_____

_____

FOCUSING YOUR THOUGHTS

Fix your thoughts on what is true and honorable and right.
Think about things that are pure and lovely and admirable.
Think about things that are excellent and worthy of praise.

Philippians 4:8 NLT

If you've ever been plagued by intense feelings of sadness, nobody needs to tell you that thoughts are intensely powerful things—you know from personal experience.

Our thoughts have the power to lift us up or drag us down; they have the power to energize us or deplete us, to inspire us to greater accomplishments, or to make those accomplishments impossible.

Bishop Fulton Sheen correctly observed, "The mind is like a clock that is constantly running down. It needs to be wound up daily with good thoughts." But sometimes, even for the most faithful believers, winding up our intellectual clocks is difficult indeed. Difficult, but necessary.

So if negative feelings have left you worried, exhausted, or both, it's time to readjust your thought patterns by training yourself to focus more on God's power and on your own possibilities. Both are far greater than you can imagine.

—Your Thoughts for Today—

A SACRIFICIAL LOVE

I am the good shepherd. The good shepherd lays down his life for the sheep.

John 10:11 Holman CSB

How much does Christ love us? More than we, as mere mortals, can comprehend. His love is perfect and steadfast. Even though we are fallible and wayward, the Shepherd cares for us still. Even though we have fallen far short of the Father's commandments, Christ loves us with a power and depth that is beyond our understanding. The sacrifice that Jesus made upon the cross was made for each of us, and His love endures to the edge of eternity and beyond.

Christ's love changes everything. When you accept His gift of grace, you are transformed, not only for today, but also for all eternity. If you haven't already done so, accept Jesus Christ as your Savior. He's waiting patiently for you to invite Him into your heart. Please don't make Him wait a single minute longer.

———

We shall find in Christ enough of everything we need—for the body, for the mind, and for the spirit—to do what He wants us to do as long as He wants us to do it.

Vance Havner

—Your Thoughts for Today—

_____

_____

_____

_____

THE POWER OF PRAYER

The intense prayer of the righteous is very powerful.

James 5:16 Holman CSB

The quality of your spiritual life will be in direct proportion to the quality of your prayer life. Prayer changes things, and it changes you. Today, instead of turning things over in your mind, turn them over to God in prayer. Instead of worrying about your next decision, ask God to lead the way. Begin your prayers early in the morning and continue them throughout the day. And remember this: God does answer your prayers, but He's not likely to answer those prayers until you've prayed them.

Each time, before you pray, be quiet first and worship God in His glory. Think of what He can do and how He delights to hear the prayers of His redeemed people. Think of your place and privilege in Christ, and expect great things!

Andrew Murray

—Your Thoughts for Today—

DILIGENCE NOW

Do not lack diligence; be fervent in spirit; serve the Lord.
Romans 12:11 Holman CSB

God's Word reminds us again and again that our Creator expects us to lead disciplined lives. God doesn't reward apathy or sloth. To the contrary, He expects believers to behave with dignity and discipline.

Life's great successes seldom fall into our laps; to the contrary, our greatest accomplishments usually require work, sweat, and tears, which is perfectly fine with God. After all, He knows that we're up to the task, and He has important plans for us. May we, as disciplined believers, always be worthy of those plans.

True willpower and courage are not only on the battlefield, but also in everyday conquests over our inertia, laziness, and boredom.

D. L. Moody

—Your Thoughts for Today—

ENTHUSIASTIC DISCIPLESHIP

Do your work with enthusiasm. Work as if you were serving the Lord, not as if you were serving only men and women.

Ephesians 6:7 NCV

With whom will you choose to walk as you make the journey through and beyond your illness? Will you walk with the Son of God? Jesus walks with you. Hopefully, you will choose to walk with Him today and every day of your life.

Jesus doesn't want you to be a run-of-the-mill, follow-the-crowd kind of person. Jesus wants you to be a "new creation" through Him. And that's exactly what you should want for yourself, too. Jesus deserves your extreme enthusiasm; the world deserves it; and you deserve the experience of sharing it.

To walk out of His will is to walk into nowhere.

C. S. Lewis

—Your Thoughts for Today—

THE POWER OF WORDS

Watch the way you talk. Let nothing foul or dirty come out of your mouth. Say only what helps, each word a gift.

Ephesians 4:29 MSG

The words that we speak have the power to do great good or great harm. If we speak words of encouragement and hope, we can lift others up. And that's exactly what God commands us to do!

Sometimes, when we feel uplifted and secure, it is easy to speak kind words. Other times, when we are discouraged or tired, we can scarcely summon the energy to uplift ourselves, much less anyone else. God intends that we speak words of kindness, wisdom, and truth, no matter our circumstances, no matter our emotions. When we do, we share a priceless gift with the world, and we give glory to the One who gave His life for us. As believers, we must do no less.

———

It is helpful to remember the distinction between appreciation and affirmation. We appreciate what a person does, but we affirm who a person is.

Charles Swindoll

—Your Thoughts for Today—

_____

_____

_____

_____

_____

AN INTENSELY BRIGHT FUTURE: YOURS

I came so they can have real and eternal life, more and better life than they ever dreamed of.

John 10:10 MSG

Do you confidently expect God to lead you to a place of abundance, peace, and joy? And, when your days on earth are over, do you expect to receive the priceless gift of eternal life? If you trust God's promises, and if you have welcomed God's Son into your heart, then you believe that your future is intensely and eternally bright.

It takes courage to dream big dreams. You will discover that courage when you do three things: accept the past, trust God to handle the future, and make the most of the time He has given you today. No dreams are too big for God—not even yours. So start living—and dreaming—accordingly.

The Christian believes in a fabulous future.

Billy Graham

—Your Thoughts for Today—

_____

_____

_____

_____

_____

TEMPORARY SETBACKS

So you also have sorrow now. But I will see you again. Your hearts will rejoice, and no one will rob you of your joy.

John 16:22 Holman CSB

In life, occasional disappointments are inevitable. Our setbacks are simply the price we pay for being human. But even when we encounter bitter disappointments, we must never lose faith.

When we encounter the challenges of life-here-on-earth, God stands ready to protect us. Our responsibility, of course, is to ask Him for protection. When we call upon Him in heartfelt prayer, He will answer—in His own time and according to His own plan—and He will heal us. And, while we are waiting for God's plans to unfold and for His healing touch to restore us, we can be comforted in the knowledge that our Creator can overcome any obstacle, even if we cannot.

The next time you're disappointed, don't panic. Don't give up. Just be patient and let God remind you he's still in control.

Max Lucado

—Your Thoughts for Today—

_____

_____

_____

_____

_____

AN AWESOME GOD

The fear of the Lord is a fountain of life, turning people from the snares of death.

Proverbs 14:27 Holman CSB

God's hand shapes the universe, and it shapes our lives. God maintains absolute sovereignty over His creation, and His power is beyond comprehension. As believers, we must cultivate a sincere respect for God's awesome power. God has dominion over all things, and until we acknowledge His sovereignty, we lack the humility we need to live righteously, and we lack the humility we need to become wise.

The fear of the Lord is, indeed, the beginning of knowledge. So today, as you face the realities of your journey through life, remember this: until you acquire a healthy, respectful fear of God's power, your education is incomplete, and so is your faith.

The fear of God is the death of every other fear.

C. H. *Spurgeon*

—Your Thoughts for Today—

_____

_____

_____

_____

_____

_____

DECISION-MAKING 101

An indecisive man is unstable in all his ways.

James 1:8 Holman CSB

From the instant you wake in the morning until the moment you nod off to sleep at night, you have the opportunity to make countless decisions: decisions about the things you do, decisions about the words you speak, and decisions about the thoughts you choose to think.

If you're facing one of life's major decisions, here are some things you can do: 1. Gather as much information as you can. 2. Don't be too impulsive. 3. Rely on the advice of trusted friends, mentors, and professionals. 4. Pray for guidance. 5. Trust the quiet inner voice of your conscience. 6. When the time for action arrives, act. Procrastination is the enemy of progress; don't let it defeat you. So when in doubt, be decisive. It's the decent way to live.

There is no need to fear the decisions of life when you know Jesus Christ, for His name is Counselor.

Warren Wiersbe

—Your Thoughts for Today—

_____

_____

_____

_____

_____

COMPLETE JOY

I have spoken these things to you so that My joy may be in you and your joy may be complete.

John 15:11 Holman CSB

Oswald Chambers correctly observed, "Joy is the great note all throughout the Bible." But, even the most dedicated Christians can, on occasion, forget to celebrate. After all, the journey through any significant illness is a difficult, daunting journey.

Every day, even if it's a difficult day, is a priceless gift from above. So even if you're not feeling your best, put a smile on your face. Keep God's love in your heart and kind words on your lips. Then, as you continue on the journey through and beyond your illness, your ability to find happiness—and to share it—will show the world just what it means to be a joyful Christian.

Joy cannot be pursued. It comes from within. It is a state of being. It does not depend on circumstances, but triumphs over circumstances.

Billy Graham

—Your Thoughts for Today—

_____

_____

_____

_____

_____

_____

GOD WANTS TO USE YOU

To everything there is a season, a time for every purpose under heaven.

Ecclesiastes 3:1 NKJV

God has things He wants you to do and lessons He wants you to share. You may be certain that God is planning to use your experiences in surprising ways. And you may be certain that He intends to lead you along a path of His choosing. Your task is to watch for His signs, to listen to His words, to obey His commandments, and to follow where He leads.

Can you use your own hardships to help others? Of course you can; of course you should. And, the best day to begin is this day.

In God's economy, whether He is making a flower or a human soul, nothing ever comes to nothing. The losses are His way of accomplishing the gains.

Elisabeth Elliot

—Your Thoughts for Today—

_____

_____

_____

_____

_____

_____

PRAISE HIM

Praise the Lord! Oh, give thanks to the Lord, for He is good!
For His mercy endures forever.

Psalm 106:1 NKJV

Sometimes, especially if our thoughts are focused on illness and recovery, we may not slow down long enough to pause and thank our Creator for the countless blessings He has bestowed upon us. But when we slow down and express our gratitude to the One who made us, we enrich our own lives and the lives of those around us.

Thanksgiving should become a habit, a regular part of our daily routines. God has blessed us beyond measure, and we owe Him everything, including our eternal praise. Let us praise Him today, tomorrow, and throughout eternity.

Most of the verses written about praise in God's Word were voiced by people faced with crushing heartaches, injustice, treachery, slander, and scores of other difficult situations.

Joni Eareckson Tada

—Your Thoughts for Today—

DOERS OF THE WORD

But be doers of the word and not hearers only.

James 1:22 Holman CSB

The old saying is both familiar and true: actions speak louder than words. And as believers, we must beware: our actions should always give credence to the changes that Christ can make in the lives of those who walk with Him.

God calls upon each of us to act in accordance with His will and with respect for His commandments. If we are to be responsible believers, we must realize that it is never enough simply to hear the instructions of God; we must also live by them. And it is never enough to wait idly by while others do God's work here on earth; we, too, must act. Doing God's work is a responsibility that each of us must bear, and when we do, our loving Heavenly Father rewards our efforts with a bountiful harvest.

Action springs not from thought, but from a readiness for responsibility.

Dietrich Bonhoeffer

—Your Thoughts for Today—

CHOOSING THE GOOD LIFE

And in that day you will ask Me nothing. Most assuredly, I say to you, whatever you ask the Father in My name He will give you. Until now you have asked nothing in My name. Ask, and you will receive, that your joy may be full.

John 16:23-24 NKJV

God offers us abundance through His Son, Jesus. Whether or not we accept God's abundance is, of course, up to each of us. When we entrust our hearts and our days to the One who created us, we experience abundance through the grace and sacrifice of His Son, Jesus. But, when we turn our thoughts and our energies away from God's commandments, we inevitably forfeit the spiritual abundance that might otherwise be ours.

If you sincerely seek the spiritual abundance that your Savior offers, then follow Him completely and without reservation. When you do, you will receive the love, the life, and the abundance that He has promised.

———————

Jesus wants Life for us, Life with a capital L.

John Eldredge

—Your Thoughts for Today—

_____

_____

_____

_____

_____

STANDING ON THE ROCK

He heals the brokenhearted and binds up their wounds.
Psalm 147:3 Holman CSB

God loves us and protects us. In times of trouble, He comforts us; in times of sorrow, He dries our tears. Psalm 147 promises, "He heals the brokenhearted, and binds their wounds" (v. 3, NASB). When we are troubled, we must call upon God, and—in His own time and according to His own plan—He will heal us.

Do you feel fearful, or weak, or sorrowful? Are you discouraged or bitter? Do you feel "stuck" in a place that is uncomfortable for you? If so, remember that God is as near as your next breath. So trust Him and turn to Him for solace, for security, and for salvation. And build your life on the rock that cannot be shaken . . . that rock is God.

God will never let you sink under your circumstances. He always provides a safety net and His love always encircles.

Barbara Johnson

—Your Thoughts for Today—

_____

_____

_____

_____

_____

A PRICELESS TREASURE

Man shall not live by bread alone, but by every word that proceeds from the mouth of God.

Matthew 4:4 NKJV

The Bible is a priceless gift, a tool for Christians to use as they share the Good News of their Savior, Christ Jesus. Too many Christians, however, keep their spiritual tool kits tightly closed and out of sight.

Jonathan Edwards advised, "Be assiduous in reading the Holy Scriptures. This is the fountain whence all knowledge in divinity must be derived. Therefore let not this treasure lie by you neglected."

God's Holy Word is, indeed, a priceless, one-of-a-kind treasure. Handle it with care, but more importantly, handle it every day . . . starting today.

The Bible is the treasure map that leads us to God's highest treasure: eternal life.

Max Lucado

—Your Thoughts for Today—

_____

_____

_____

_____

_____

_____

WHAT DOESN'T CHANGE

Jesus Christ is the same yesterday, today, and forever.
Hebrews 13:8 Holman CSB

Our world is in a state of constant change. God is not. At times, the world seems to be trembling beneath our feet. But we can be comforted in the knowledge that our Heavenly Father is the rock that cannot be shaken. His Word promises, "I am the Lord, I do not change" (Malachi 3:6 NKJV).

Every day that we live, we mortals encounter a multitude of changes—some good, some not so good, some downright disheartening. On those occasions when we must endure life-changing personal losses that leave us breathless, there is a place we can turn for comfort and assurance—we can turn to God. When we do, our loving Heavenly Father stands ready to protect us, to comfort us, to guide us, and, in time, to heal us.

In a world kept chaotic by change, you will eventually discover, as I have, that this is one of the most precious qualities of the God we are looking for: He doesn't change.

Bill Hybels

—Your Thoughts for Today—

ULTIMATE ACCOUNTABILITY

We encouraged, comforted, and implored each one of you to walk worthy of God, who calls you into His own kingdom and glory.

1 Thessalonians 2:12 Holman CSB

For most of us, it is a daunting thought: one day, perhaps soon, we'll come face-to-face with our Heavenly Father, and we'll be called to account for our actions here on earth. Our personal histories will certainly not be surprising to God; He already knows everything about us. But the full scope of our activities may be surprising to us: some of us will be pleasantly surprised; others will not be.

Today, do whatever you can to ensure that your thoughts and your deeds are pleasing to your Creator. Because you will, at some point in the future, be called to account for your actions. When you're faced with a difficult choice or a powerful temptation, seek God's counsel and trust the counsel He gives. Invite God into your heart and live according to His commandments. When you do, you will be blessed today, and tomorrow, and forever.

Our walk counts far more than our talk, always!

George Mueller

—Your Thoughts for Today—

_____

_____

_____

LIVING IN AN ANXIOUS WORLD

Cast all your anxiety on him because he cares for you.
1 Peter 5:7 NIV

We live in a world that often breeds anxiety and fear. When we come face-to-face with tough times, we may fall prey to discouragement, doubt, or depression. But our Father in heaven has other plans. God has promised that we may lead lives of abundance, not anxiety. In fact, His Word instructs us to "be anxious for nothing" (Philippians 4:6). But how can we put our fears to rest? By taking those fears to God and leaving them there.

As you face the challenges of your illness, you may find yourself becoming anxious, troubled, discouraged, or fearful. If so, turn every one of your concerns over to your Heavenly Father. The same God who created the universe will comfort you if you ask Him…so ask Him and trust Him. And then watch in amazement as your anxieties melt into the warmth of His loving hands.

One of the main missions of God is to free us from the debilitating bonds of fear and anxiety. God's heart is broken when He sees us so demoralized and weighed down by fear.

Bill Hybels

—Your Thoughts for Today—

YOUR PLANS AND GOD'S PLANS

A man's heart plans his way, but the Lord determines his steps.

Proverbs 16:9 Holman CSB

If you're like most people, you like being in control. Period. You want things to happen according to your wishes and according to your timetable. But sometimes, God has other plans . . . and He always has the final word. Are you embittered by an illness that you did not deserve and cannot understand? If so, it's time to make peace with life. It's time to forgive others, and, if necessary, to forgive yourself. It's time to accept the unchangeable past, to embrace the priceless present, and to have faith in the promise of tomorrow. It's time to trust God completely. And it's time to reclaim the peace—His peace—that can and should be yours.

Acceptance is resting in God's goodness, believing that He has all things under His control.

Charles Swindoll

—Your Thoughts for Today—

_____

_____

_____

_____

_____

_____

_____

SMILE

Rejoice in the Lord, you righteous ones; praise from the upright is beautiful.

Psalm 33:1 Holman CSB

A smile is nourishment for the heart, and laughter is medicine for the soul—but sometimes, amid the stresses of the day, we forget to take our medicine. Instead of viewing our world with a mixture of optimism and humor, we allow worries and distractions to rob us of the joy that God intends for our lives.

So the next time you find yourself dwelling upon the negatives of life, refocus your attention to things positive. The next time you find yourself falling prey to the blight of pessimism, stop yourself and turn your thoughts around. With a loving God as your protector, and with a loving family to support you, you're blessed now and forever. So smile . . . starting now!

Any man can sing in the day. It is easy to sing when we can read the notes by daylight, but he is the skillful singer who can sing when there is not a ray of light by which to read. Songs in the night come only from God; they are not in the power of man.

C. H. Spurgeon

—Your Thoughts for Today—

OFFERING THANKS

In everything give thanks; for this is the will of God in Christ Jesus for you.

1 Thessalonians 5:18 NKJV

Life with a serious illness can be complicated, demanding, and frustrating. When the demands of life leave you rushing from place to place with scarcely a moment to spare, you may fail to pause and thank the Creator for His gifts.

Today, begin making a list of your blessings. You most certainly will not be able to make a complete list, but take a few moments and jot down as many blessings as you can. Then, give thanks to the Giver of all good things: God. His love for you is eternal, as are His gifts. And it's never too soon—or too late—to offer Him thanks.

In times of affliction, we commonly meet with the sweetest experiences of the love of God.

John Bunyan

—Your Thoughts for Today—

SAYING YES TO GOD

Cast your burden on the Lord, and He will support you; He will never allow the righteous to be shaken.

Psalm 55:22 Holman CSB

Your decision to seek a deeper relationship with God will not remove all problems from your life; to the contrary, it will bring about a series of personal crises as you constantly seek to say "yes" to God although the world encourages you to do otherwise. You live in a world that seeks to snare your attention and lead you away from God. Each time you are tempted to distance yourself from the Creator, you will face a spiritual crisis. A few of these crises may be monumental in scope, but most will be the small, everyday decisions of life. In fact, life here on earth can be seen as one test after another—and with each crisis comes yet another opportunity to grow closer to God . . . or to distance yourself from His plan for your life.

Today, as you continue the journey through and beyond your illness, you will face many opportunities to say "yes" to your Creator—and you will also encounter many opportunities to say "no" to Him. Your answers will determine the quality of your day and the direction of your life, so answer carefully . . . very carefully.

—Your Thoughts for Today—

_____

_____

_____

_____

PATIENCE AND THE PATIENT

Do everything without complaining or arguing. Then you will be innocent and without any wrong.

Philippians 2:14-15 NCV

Treating and defeating cancer is serious business. The life of a cancer patient can be a hard life, indeed. So there's plenty of room—and plenty of reason—to complain. But complaints often do more damage than good: damage to others and damage to ourselves.

So the next time you're tempted to complain about something great or small, slow down, calm down, and take a few moments to ask God how you should respond. If you listen carefully to God, you may discover that He wants you to be a more patient patient.

———◆◆◆———

Jesus wept, but he never complained.

C. H. Spurgeon

—Your Thoughts for Today—

_____

_____

_____

_____

_____

_____

_____

BE STILL

Be still, and know that I am God.

Psalm 46:10 NKJV

Do you take time each day for an extended period of silence? And during those precious moments, do you sincerely open your heart to your Creator? If so, you are wise and you are blessed.

The world can be a noisy place, a place filled to the brim with distractions, interruptions, and frustrations. And if you're not careful, the struggles and stresses of life can rob you of the peace that could be yours through Christ. So take time each day to quietly commune with your Savior. When you do, those moments of silence will enable you to participate more fully in the only source of peace that endures: God's peace.

———

Growth takes place in quietness, in hidden ways, in silence and solitude.

Eugene Peterson

—Your Thoughts for Today—

_____

_____

_____

_____

_____

_____

ALWAYS LEARNING
ABOUT JESUS

I want their hearts to be encouraged and joined together in love, so that they may have all the riches of assured understanding, and have the knowledge of God's mystery—Christ.

Colossians 2:2 Holman CSB

As Christians, we can—and should—never stop growing in the love and knowledge of our Savior.

When we cease to grow, either emotionally or spiritually, we do ourselves and our loved ones a profound disservice. But, if we study God's Word, if we obey His commandments, and if we live in the center of His will, we will not be "stagnant" believers; we will, instead, be growing Christians . . . and that's exactly what God wants for our lives and our relationships.

So Jesus came, stripping himself of everything as he came—omnipotence, omniscience, omnipresence—everything except love. "He emptied himself" (Philippians 2:7), emptied himself of everything except love. Love—his only protection, his only weapon, his only method.

E. Stanley Jones

—Your Thoughts for Today—

_____

_____

_____

LOVING GOD

We love him, because he first loved us.

1 John 4:19 KJV

When we worship God with faith and assurance, and when we place Him at the absolute center of our lives, we invite His love into our hearts. In turn, we grow to love Him more deeply as we sense His love for us. St. Augustine wrote, "I love you, Lord, not doubtingly, but with absolute certainty. Your Word beat upon my heart until I fell in love with you, and now the universe and everything in it tells me to love you." Let us pray that we, too, will turn our hearts to our Father, knowing with certainty that He loves us and that we love Him.

We—or at least I—shall not be able to adore God on the highest occasions if we have learned no habit of doing so on the lowest.

C. S. Lewis

—Your Thoughts for Today—

_____

_____

_____

_____

_____

_____

_____

UNDER (AND OVER) THE CIRCUMSTANCES

I have learned to be content in whatever circumstances I am.
Philippians 4:11 Holman CSB

You've probably heard it said on many occasions. Perhaps you've even said it yourself: "I'm doing the best I can under the circumstances." But God has a better way. He wants you to live above your circumstances—and with His help, you can most certainly do it.

In Philippians, Paul stated that he could find happiness and fulfillment in any situation. How? By turning His life and his future over to God. Even when he faced enormous difficulties, Paul found peace through God. So can you.

Today, make this important promise to yourself and to your Creator: Promise to rise far above your circumstances. You deserve no less . . . and neither, for that matter, does your Father in heaven.

God doesn't always change the circumstances, but He can change us to meet the circumstances. That's what it means to live by faith.

Warren Wiersbe

—Your Thoughts for Today—

A WING AND A PRAYER

Be cheerful. Keep things in good repair. Keep your spirits up. Think in harmony. Be agreeable. Do all that, and the God of love and peace will be with you for sure.

2 Corinthians 13:11 MSG

Mrs. Charles E. Cowman, the author of the classic devotional text, *Streams in the Desert*, wrote, "Two wings are necessary to lift our souls toward God: prayer and praise. Prayer asks. Praise accepts the answer." That's why we should find the time to lift our concerns to God in prayer, and to praise Him for all that He has done.

John Wesley correctly observed, "Sour godliness is the devil's religion." These words remind us that pessimism and doubt are some of the most important tools that Satan uses to achieve his objectives. Our challenge, of course, is to ensure that Satan cannot use these tools on us.

———

Christ can put a spring in your step and a thrill in your heart. Optimism and cheerfulness are products of knowing Christ.

Billy Graham

—Your Thoughts for Today—

_____

_____

_____

_____

_____

A GROWING RELATIONSHIP WITH GOD

But grow in the grace and knowledge of our Lord and Savior Jesus Christ. To Him be the glory both now and to the day of eternity.

2 Peter 3:18 Holman CSB

Your relationship with God is ongoing; it unfolds day by day, and it offers countless opportunities to grow closer to Him . . . or not. As each new day unfolds, you are confronted with a wide range of decisions: how you will behave, where you will direct your thoughts, with whom you will associate, and what you will choose to worship.

Are you continuing to grow in your love and knowledge of the Lord, or are you "satisfied" with the current state of your spiritual health? Hopefully, you're determined to make yourself a growing Christian. Your Savior deserves no less, and neither, by the way, do you.

When it comes to walking with God, there is no such thing as instant maturity. God doesn't mass produce His saints. He hand tools each one, and it always takes longer than we expected.

Charles Swindoll

—Your Thoughts for Today—

_____

_____

_____

_____

ARGUMENTS LOST

It is honorable for a man to resolve a dispute, but any fool can get himself into a quarrel.

Proverbs 20:3 Holman CSB

Arguments are seldom won but often lost. When we engage in petty squabbles, our losses usually outpace our gains. When we acquire the unfortunate habit of habitual bickering, we do harm to our spouses, to our friends, to our families, to our coworkers, and to ourselves.

Time and again, God's Word warns us that most arguments are a monumental waste of time, of energy, of life.

So the next time you're tempted to engage in a silly squabble, whether at home, at church, at the doctor's office, or just about anyplace else, refrain. Avoid anguished outpourings. Suppress your impulsive outbursts. Curb the need to criticize. Terminate tantrums. Learn to speak words that lift others up as you share a message of encouragement and hope to a world that needs both.

Whatever you do when conflicts arise, be wise. Fight against jumping to quick conclusions and seeing only your side. There are always two sides on the streets of conflict. Look both ways.

Charles Swindoll

—Your Thoughts for Today—

_____

_____

_____

A ONE-OF-A-KIND TREASURE

Every word of God is pure; He is a shield to those who put their trust in Him.

Proverbs 30:5 NKJV

God's Word is a roadmap for life here on earth and for life eternal. As Christians, we are called upon to study God's Holy Word, to trust its promises, to follow its commandments, and to share its Good News with the world.

As believers, we must study the Bible and meditate upon its meaning for our lives. Otherwise, we deprive ourselves of a priceless gift from our Creator. God's Holy Word is, indeed, a transforming, life-changing, one-of-a-kind treasure. And, a passing acquaintance with the Good Book is insufficient for Christians who seek to obey God's Word and to understand His will. After all, neither man nor woman should live by bread alone . . .

The Gospel is not so much a demand as it is an offer, an offer of new life to man by the grace of God.

E. Stanley Jones

—Your Thoughts for Today—

THE VOICE OF GOD

Be silent before Me.

Isaiah 41:1 Holman CSB

Sometimes God speaks loudly and clearly. More often, He speaks in a quiet voice—and if you are wise, you will be listening carefully when He does. To do so, you must carve out quiet moments each day to study His Word and sense His direction.

Can you quiet yourself long enough to listen to your conscience? Are you attuned to the subtle guidance of your intuition? Are you willing to pray sincerely and then to wait quietly for God's response. Hopefully so. Usually God refrains from sending His messages on stone tablets or city billboards. More often, He communicates in subtler ways. If you sincerely desire to hear His voice, you must listen carefully, and you must do so in the silent corners of your quiet, willing heart.

In the soul-searching of our lives, we are to stay quiet so we can hear Him say all that He wants to say to us in our hearts.

Charles Swindoll

—Your Thoughts for Today—

REAL REPENTANCE

I preached to those in Damascus first, and to those in Jerusalem and in all the region of Judea, and to the Gentiles, that they should repent and turn to God, and do works worthy of repentance.

Acts 26:20 Holman CSB

Who among us has sinned? All of us. But the good news is this: When we do ask God's forgiveness and turn our hearts to Him, He forgives us absolutely and completely.

Genuine repentance requires more than simply offering God apologies for our misdeeds. Real repentance may start with feelings of sorrow and remorse, but it ends only when we turn away from the sin that has heretofore distanced us from our Creator. In truth, we offer our most meaningful apologies to God, not with our words, but with our actions. As long as we are still engaged in sin, we may be "repenting," but we have not fully "repented." So, if there is an aspect of your life that is distancing you from your God, ask for His forgiveness, and—just as importantly—stop sinning. Now.

Repentance involves a radical change of heart and mind in which we agree with God's evaluation of our sin and then take specific action to align ourselves with His will.

Henry Blackaby

—Your Thoughts for Today—

_____

_____

_____

LOOKING FOR OPPORTUNITIES

But if we look forward to something we don't have yet, we must wait patiently and confidently.

Romans 8:25 NLT

As you look at the landscape of your life, do you see opportunities, possibilities, and blessings, or do you focus, instead, upon the more negative scenery? Do you spend more time counting your blessings or your misfortunes? If you've acquired the unfortunate habit of focusing too intently upon the negative aspects of your life, then your spiritual vision is in need of correction.

The way that you choose to view the scenery around you will have a profound impact on the quality, the tone, and the direction of your life. The more you focus on the beauty that surrounds you, the more beautiful your own life becomes.

We don't give up. We look up. We trust. We believe. And our optimism is not hollow. Christ has proven worthy. He has shown that he never fails.

Max Lucado

—Your Thoughts for Today—

BEYOND ANGER AND GUILT

Refrain from anger and give up [your] rage; do not be agitated—it can only bring harm.

Psalm 37:8 Holman CSB

Anger, left unchecked, tends to invade every aspect of life, eventually transforming itself into bitterness. Irrational guilt, especially over past events that cannot be changed, creates an environment of self-doubt and self-recrimination.

If you are ruled by feelings of anger, guilt, jealousy, fear, or any other negative emotion, understand that these emotions are part of the grieving process. But understand too that hurtful feelings should never become a permanent part of your emotional makeup. God has better things in store for you!

Acrid bitterness inevitably seeps into the lives of people who harbor grudges and suppress anger, and bitterness is always a poison.

Lee Strobel

—Your Thoughts for Today—

GUARD YOUR HEART

The peace of God, which surpasses all understanding, will guard your hearts and minds through Christ Jesus.

Philippians 4:7 NKJV

Y ou are near and dear to God. He loves you more than you can imagine, and He wants the very best for you. And one more thing: God wants you to guard your heart.

Every day, you are faced with choices . . . more choices than you can count. You can do the right thing, or not. You can be prudent, or not. You can be kind, and generous, and obedient to God. Or not.

Today, the world will offer you countless opportunities to let down your guard and, by doing so, make needless mistakes that may injure you or your loved ones. So be watchful and obedient. Guard your heart by giving it to your Heavenly Father; it is safe with Him.

The more wisdom enters our hearts, the more we will be able to trust our hearts in difficult situations.

John Eldredge

—Your Thoughts for Today—

_____

_____

_____

_____

_____

_____

GOD SEES THE HEART

For God will bring every act to judgment, including every hidden thing, whether good or evil.

Ecclesiastes 12:14 Holman CSB

If you wish to be honored by your peers, you must lead a life that appears to be honorable. But, if you seek honor from God, you must not only behave honorably, you must also be motivated by righteous intentions. Why? Because God knows your heart.

Whom will you try to please today: God or man? Your obligation is most certainly not to imperfect men or women. Your obligation is to an all-knowing and perfect God. Trust Him always. Love Him always. Praise Him always. Seek to please Him and only Him. Always. And then, receive the only honor that really counts: His.

———

Whenever you are tempted to the commission of any sin, or the omission of any duty, pause and say to yourself, What am I about to do? God sees me.

Susanna Wesley

—Your Thoughts for Today—

_____

_____

_____

_____

_____

_____

_____

THE ANSWER TO ADVERSITY

I have heard your prayer, I have seen your tears; surely I will heal you.

From time to time, all of us must endure tough times. And, we sometimes experience life-changing personal losses that leave us reeling. When we do, God stands ready to protect us. When we are troubled, we must call upon God, and, in His own time and according to His own plan, He will heal us.

Are you anxious about your illness? Take those anxieties to God. Seek protection from the One who cannot be moved. The same God who created the universe will protect you if you ask Him . . . so ask Him. Right now.

Measure the size of the obstacles against the size of God.

Beth Moore

—Your Thoughts for Today—

_____

_____

_____

_____

_____

_____

_____

_____

WHEN HOPE IS IN
SHORT SUPPLY

I wait for the Lord; I wait, and put my hope in His word.

Psalm 130:5 Holman CSB

Sometimes, hope can be a highly perishable commodity. When the challenges and pressures of everyday life threaten to overwhelm us, we may convince ourselves that the future holds little promise—and we may allow our fears to eclipse our dreams.

When hope seems to be in short supply, there is a source to which we can turn in order to restore our perspective and our strength. That source is God. When we lift our prayers to the Creator, we avail ourselves of God's power, God's wisdom, and God's love. And when we allow God's Son to reign over our hearts, we are transformed, not just for a day, but for all eternity.

Are you looking for a renewed sense of hope? If so, it's time to place your future in the loving hands of God's only begotten Son. When you do, you'll discover that hope is not only highly perishable, but that it is also readily renewable . . . one day—and one moment—at a time.

If your hopes are being disappointed just now, it means that they are being purified.

Oswald Chambers

Everything that is done in the world is done by hope.

Martin Luther

The popular idea of faith is of a certain obstinate optimism: the hope, tenaciously held in the face of trouble, that the universe is fundamentally friendly and things may get better.

J. I. Packer

When the hard times of life come, we know that no matter how tragic the circumstances seem, no matter how long the spiritual drought, no matter how long and dark the days, the sun is sure to break through; the dawn will come.

Gloria Gaither

Our heavenly Father never takes anything from his children unless he means to give them something better.

George Mueller

—Your Thoughts for Today—

WORSHIP AND PRAISE

But an hour is coming, and is now here, when the true worshipers will worship the Father in spirit and truth. Yes, the Father wants such people to worship Him. God is Spirit, and those who worship Him must worship in spirit and truth.

John 4:23-24 Holman CSB

Where do we worship? In our hearts or in our church? The answer is both. As Christians who have been saved by a loving, compassionate Creator, we are compelled not only to worship the Creator in our hearts but also to worship Him in the presence of fellow believers.

We live in a world that is teeming with temptations and distractions—a world where good and evil struggle in a constant battle to win our hearts and souls. Our challenge, of course, is to ensure that we cast our lot on the side of God. One way to ensure that we do so is by the practice of regular, purposeful worship with our families. So as you move through and beyond your illness, make worship a cornerstone of your recovery. Let God's transcendent love surround you and transform you, today and every day.

—Your Thoughts for Today—

_____

_____

_____

_____

_____

BEYOND WORRY

The one who understands a matter finds success, and the one who trusts in the Lord will be happy.

Proverbs 16:20 Holman CSB

Because we are imperfect human beings, we worry. Even though we are Christians who have been given the assurance of salvation—even though we are Christians who have received the promise of God's love and protection—we find ourselves fretting over the countless details of everyday life. Jesus understood our concerns when He spoke the reassuring words found in Matthew 6: "Therefore I tell you, do not worry about your life . . ."

God is the Rock that cannot be moved. When you build your life upon that Rock, you have absolutely no need to worry . . . not now, not ever.

The secret of Christian quietness is not indifference, but the knowledge that God is my Father, He loves me, and that I shall never think of anything He will forget. Then, worry becomes an impossibility.

Oswald Chambers

—Your Thoughts for Today—

_____

_____

_____

_____

_____

A TIME TO REST

Are you tired? Worn out? Burned out on religion? Come to me. Get away with me and you'll recover your life. I'll show you how to take a real rest. Walk with me and work with me...watch how I do it. Learn the unforced rhythms of grace. I won't lay anything heavy or ill-fitting on you. Keep company with me and you'll learn to live freely and lightly.

Matthew 11:28-30 MSG

Sometimes, the struggles of life can drain us of our strength. When we find ourselves tired, discouraged, or worse, there is a source from which we can draw the power needed to recharge our spiritual batteries. That source, of course, is God.

God expects us to work hard, but He also intends for us to rest. When we fail to take the rest that we need, we do a disservice to ourselves and to our families.

Is your spiritual battery running low? Is your energy on the wane? Are your emotions frayed? If so, it's time to turn your thoughts and your prayers to God. And when you're finished, it's time to rest.

Life is strenuous. See that your clock does not run down.

Mrs. Charles E. Cowman

—Your Thoughts for Today—

_____

_____

_____

_____

_____

LIFETIME LEARNING

Accept my instruction instead of silver, and knowledge rather than pure gold. For wisdom is better than precious stones, and nothing desirable can compare with it.

Proverbs 8:10-11 Holman CSB

Today is your classroom: what will you learn? Will you use today's experiences as tools for personal growth, or will you ignore the lessons that life and God are trying to teach you? Will you carefully study God's Word, and will you apply His teachings to the experiences of everyday life? The events of today have much to teach. You have much to learn. May you live—and learn—accordingly.

The process of living seems to consist in coming to realize truths so ancient and simple that, if stated, they sound like barren platitudes. They cannot sound otherwise to those who have not had the relevant experience.

C. S. Lewis

—Your Thoughts for Today—

_____

_____

_____

_____

_____

_____

HE RENEWS OUR STRENGTH

Have you not known? Have you not heard? The everlasting God, the Lord, the Creator of the ends of the earth, neither faints nor is weary. His understanding is unsearchable. He gives power to the weak, and to those who have no might He increases strength.

Isaiah 40:28-29 NKJV

When we genuinely lift our hearts and prayers to God, He renews our strength. Are you almost too weary to lift your head? Then bow it. Offer your concerns and your fears to your Father in heaven. He is always at your side, offering His love and His strength.

Are you troubled or anxious? Take your anxieties to God in prayer. Are you weak or worried? Delve deeply into God's Holy Word and sense His presence in the quiet moments of the day. Are you spiritually exhausted? Call upon fellow believers to support you, and call upon Christ to renew your spirit and your life. Your Savior will never let you down. To the contrary, He will always lift you up if you ask Him to. So what, dear friend, are you waiting for?

Christ came when all things were growing old. He made them new.

St. Augustine

—Your Thoughts for Today—

SHARING THE GOOD NEWS

For Christ did not send me to baptize, but to preach the gospel—not with clever words, so that the cross of Christ will not be emptied of its effect.

1 Corinthians 1:17 Holman CSB

In his second letter to Timothy, Paul offers a message to believers of every generation when he writes, "God has not given us a spirit of timidity" (1:7 NASB). Paul's meaning is crystal clear: When sharing our testimonies, we, as Christians, must be courageous, forthright, and unashamed.

We live in a world that desperately needs the healing message of Christ Jesus. Every believer, each in his or her own way, bears a personal responsibility for sharing that message. If you are a believer in Christ, you know how He has touched your heart and changed your life. Now it's your turn to share the Good News with others. And remember: today is the perfect time to share your testimony because tomorrow may quite simply be too late.

How many people have you made homesick for God?

Oswald Chambers

—Your Thoughts for Today—

ON A MISSION FOR GOD

But you are a chosen race, a royal priesthood, a holy nation, a people for His possession, so that you may proclaim the praises of the One who called you out of darkness into His marvelous light.

1 Peter 2:9 Holman CSB

Whether you realize it or not, you are on a personal mission for God. As a Christian, that mission is straightforward: Honor God, accept Christ as your personal Savior, and serve God's children. Of course, you will encounter impediments as you attempt to discover the exact nature of God's purpose for your life, but you must never lose sight of the overriding purposes that God has established for all believers. You will encounter these overriding purposes again and again as you worship your Creator and study His Word.

Every day offers countless opportunities to serve God and to worship Him. When you do so, He will bless you in miraculous ways. May you continue to seek God's will, may you trust His Word, and may you place Him where He belongs: at the very center of your life.

There is something about having endured great loss that brings purity of purpose and strength of character.

Barbara Johnson

—Your Thoughts for Today—

CONTROLLING THE ANGER

A fool gives full vent to his anger, but a wise man holds it in check.

Proverbs 29:11 Holman CSB

Whenever you're being treated for a serious illness, frustrations may begin to mount. But, just because you're frustrated doesn't mean that full-blown temper tantrum is called for. After all, when you allow yourself to become angry, you are certain to defeat only one person: yourself.

When you allow the frustrations and headaches of life to hijack your emotions, you do harm to yourself and to your loved ones. So today and every day, guard yourself against the kind of angry thinking that inevitably takes a toll on your emotions and your relationships.

When something robs you of your peace of mind, ask yourself if it is worth the energy you are expending on it. If not, then put it out of your mind in an act of discipline. Every time the thought of "it" returns, refuse it.

Kay Arthur

—Your Thoughts for Today—

TRUST HIM

It is better to take refuge in the Lord than to trust in man.

Psalm 118:8 Holman CSB

The journey through and beyond any significant illness leads us over many peaks and through many valleys. When we reach the mountaintops, we find it easy to praise God, to trust Him, and to give thanks. But, when we trudge through the dark valleys of fear and despair, trusting God is more difficult.

The next time you find your courage tested to the limit, lean upon God's promises. Trust His Son. When you are worried, anxious, or afraid, call upon Him. God can handle your troubles infinitely better than you can, so turn them over to Him. Remember that God rules both mountaintops and valleys—with limitless wisdom and love—now and forever.

———

Jesus does not say, "There is no storm." He says, "I am here, do not toss, but trust."

Vance Havner

—Your Thoughts for Today—

_____

_____

_____

_____

_____

_____

_____

REDISCOVERING GOD'S PLANS

A man's heart plans his way, but the Lord directs his steps.
Proverbs 16:9 NKJV

The journey back to health is not only a first-person tour through the highs and lows of modern medicine, it is also a spiritual journey, an awakening, a time to rethink your priorities and refocus your energies. If your illness forces you to reexamine God's plan for your life, you'll join a long list of survivors who have had a similar experience.

Sometimes, God's plans are crystal clear; sometimes they are not. So be patient, keep searching, and keep praying. If you continue to ask Him with a sincere heart, God will answer your prayers and make His plans known . . . and you'll be eternally grateful that He did.

◦──◦◦◦──◦

We do not belong to ourselves, nor should we operate independently of the Spirit of God. Now that we have been converted, we are the Lord's, and as our Master, He has every right to use us in whatever way He chooses.

Charles Swindoll

—Your Thoughts for Today—

_____

_____

_____

_____

_____

_____

THE WISDOM TO FORGIVE

Therefore, God's chosen ones, holy and loved, put on heartfelt compassion, kindness, humility, gentleness, and patience, accepting one another and forgiving one another if anyone has a complaint against another. Just as the Lord has forgiven you, so also you must forgive.

Colossians 3:12-13 Holman CSB

When people behave badly, it's hard to forgive them. How hard? Sometimes, it's very hard! But God tells us that we must forgive other people, even when we'd rather not. So, if you're angry with anybody (or if you're upset by something you yourself have done) it's now time to forgive.

God instructs you to treat other people exactly as you wish to be treated. And since you want to be forgiven for the mistakes that you make, you must be willing to extend forgiveness to other people for the mistakes that they have made. If you can't seem to forgive someone, you should keep asking God to help you until you do. And you can be sure of this: if you keep asking for God's help, He will give it.

If you're going to forgive somebody eventually, why wait?

Marie T. Freeman

—Your Thoughts for Today—

FAITH THAT WORKS

For I know that my Redeemer lives.

Job 19:25 NKJV

The work of nourishing your faith can and should be joyful work. The hours that you invest in Bible study, prayer, meditation, and worship should be times of enrichment and celebration. And, as you continue to build your life upon a foundation of faith, you will discover that the journey toward spiritual maturity lasts a lifetime. As a child of God, you are never fully "grown": instead, you can continue "growing up" every day of your life. And that's exactly what God wants you to do.

Our faith grows by expression. If we want to keep our faith, we must share it. We must act.

Billy Graham

—Your Thoughts for Today—

_____

_____

_____

_____

_____

_____

_____

_____

WAITING FOR GOD

The Lord is good to those who wait for Him, to the soul who seeks Him. It is good that one should hope and wait quietly for the salvation of the Lord.

Lamentations 3:25–26 NKJV

We human beings are so impatient. We know what we want, and we know exactly when we want it: Right now. But, God knows better. He has created a world that unfolds according to His own timetable, not ours.

As Christians, we must be patient as we wait for God to reveal the plans that He has in store for us. And while we're waiting for God to make His plans clear, let's keep praying and keep giving thanks to the One who has given us more blessings than we can count.

To wait upon God is the perfection of activity.

Oswald Chambers

—Your Thoughts for Today—

_____

_____

_____

_____

_____

_____

_____

_____

THE DIRECTION OF YOUR THOUGHTS

My cup runs over. Surely goodness and mercy shall follow me all the days of my life; and I will dwell in the house of the Lord Forever.

Psalm 23:5-6 NKJV

God has given you free will, including the ability to influence the direction and the tone of your thoughts. And, here's how God wants you to direct those thoughts: "Finally brothers, whatever is true, whatever is honorable, whatever is just, whatever is pure, whatever is lovely, whatever is commendable—if there is any moral excellence and if there is any praise—dwell on these things" (Philippians 4:8 Holman CSB).

The quality of your attitude will help determine the quality of your life, so you must guard your thoughts accordingly. So, the next time you find yourself dwelling upon the negative aspects of your illness or your life, refocus your attention on things positive. It's the right way to think and the right way to live.

Our attitude determines our approach to life.

John Maxwell

—Your Thoughts for Today—

_____

_____

_____

_____

_____

PATS ON THE BACK

So then, we must pursue what promotes peace and what builds up one another.

Romans 14:19 Holman CSB

Life is a team sport, and all of us need occasional pats on the back from our teammates. In the book of Ephesians, Paul writes, "Do not let any unwholesome talk come out of your mouths, but only what is helpful for building others up according to their needs, that it may benefit those who listen" (4:29 NIV). Paul reminds us that when we choose our words carefully, we can have a powerful impact on those around us.

Since we don't always know who needs our help, the best strategy is to encourage all the people who cross our paths. So today, be a world-class source of encouragement to everyone you meet. Never has the need been greater.

———

Make it a rule, and pray to God to help you to keep it, never to lie down at night without being able to say: "I have made at least one human being a little wiser, a little happier, or a little better this day."

Charles Kingsley

—Your Thoughts for Today—

KEEP AN ETERNAL PERSPECTIVE

If you become wise, you will be the one to benefit. If you scorn wisdom, you will be the one to suffer.

Proverbs 9:12 NLT

As you make the journey through and beyond serious illness, will you carve out quiet moments each day to offer thanksgiving and praise to your Creator? You should. During these moments of stillness, you will often sense the love and wisdom of our Lord.

The familiar words of Psalm 46:10 remind us to "Be still, and know that I am God" (NKJV). When we do so, we encounter the awesome presence of our loving Heavenly Father, and we are blessed beyond words. But, when we ignore the presence of our Creator, we rob ourselves of His perspective, His peace, and His joy.

Today and every day, make time to be still before God. When you do, you can face the day's complications with the wisdom and power that only He can provide.

God is good, and heaven is forever. These two facts should brighten up even the darkest day.

Marie T. Freeman

—Your Thoughts for Today—

SHARING THE LESSONS YOU'VE LEARNED

Based on the gift they have received, everyone should use it to serve others, as good managers of the varied grace of God.
1 Peter 4:10 Holman CSB

All people possess special insights—bestowed from the Father above—and you are no exception. Today, as you consider the landscape of your life, be sure that you're preparing yourself to share the lessons you've learned as you've journeyed through and beyond cancer.

Serious illness has a way of teaching lessons that you might not have learned in any other way. And God wants you to share those lessons with family, with friends, and with the world. So don't keep your wisdom to yourself; share your insights today, and keep sharing them as long as God gives you the power to do so.

Discouraged people don't need critics. They hurt enough already. They need encouragement. They need a refuge, a willing, caring, available someone.

Charles Swindoll

—Your Thoughts for Today—

_____

_____

_____

_____

_____

A POSITIVE INFLUENCE

Be an example to the believers in word, in conduct, in love, in spirit, in faith, in purity.

1 Timothy 4:12 NKJV

As followers of Christ, we must each ask ourselves an important question: "What kind of example am I?" The answer to that question determines, in large part, whether or not we are positive influences on our own little corners of the world.

Are you the kind of person whose life serves as a powerful example of righteousness? Are you a person whose behavior serves as a positive role model for young people? Are you the kind of Christian whose actions, day in and day out, are based upon integrity, fidelity, and a love for the Lord? If so, you are not only blessed by God, you are also a powerful force for good in a world that desperately needs positive influences such as yours.

In our faith we follow in someone's steps. In our faith we leave footprints to guide others. It's the principle of discipleship.

Max Lucado

—Your Thoughts for Today—

_____

_____

_____

_____

_____

TROUBLED TIMES

He shall not be afraid of evil tidings: his heart is fixed, trusting in the LORD.

Psalm 112:7 KJV

We live in a fear-based world, a world where bad news travels at light speed and good news doesn't. These are troubled times, times when we have legitimate fears for the future of our nation, our world, and our families. But as Christians, we have every reason to live courageously. After all, the ultimate battle has already been fought and won on that faraway cross at Calvary.

Perhaps you, like countless other believers, have found your courage tested by the anxieties and fears that are an inevitable part of 21st-century life. If so, God wants to have a little chat with you. The next time you find your courage tested to the limit, God wants to remind you that He is not just near, He is here. Your Heavenly Father is your Protector and your Deliverer. Call upon Him in your hour of need, and be comforted. Whatever your challenge, whatever your trouble, God can handle it. And will.

—Your Thoughts for Today—

_____

_____

_____

_____

THE CORNERSTONE

Let us fix our eyes on Jesus, the author and perfecter of our faith, who for the joy set before him endured the cross, scorning its shame, and sat down at the right hand of the throne of God.

Hebrews 12:2 NIV

I s Christ the focus of your life? Are you an energized Christian who allows God's Son to reign over every aspect of your day? Make no mistake: that's exactly what God intends for you to do.

God has given you the gift of eternal life through His Son. In response to God's priceless gift, you are instructed to focus your thoughts, your prayers, and your energies upon God and His only begotten Son. To do so, you must resist the subtle yet powerful temptation to become a "spiritual dabbler." A person who dabbles in the Christian faith is unwilling to place God above all other things. Resist that temptation; make God the cornerstone and the touchstone of your life. When you do, He will give you all the strength and wisdom you need to live victoriously for Him.

Jesus challenges you and me to keep our focus daily on the cross of His will if we want to be His disciples.

Anne Graham Lotz

—Your Thoughts for Today—

CONTAGIOUS FAITH

Whatever you do, do it enthusiastically, as something done for the Lord and not for men.

Colossians 3:23 Holman CSB

Genuine, heartfelt Christianity is contagious. If you enjoy a life-altering relationship with God, that relationship will have an impact on others—perhaps a profound impact.

Are you genuinely excited about your faith? And do you make your enthusiasm known to those around you? Or are you a "silent ambassador" for Christ? God's preference is clear: He intends that you stand before others and proclaim your faith.

Does Christ reign over your life? Then share your testimony and your excitement. The world needs both.

The proper perspective creates within us a spirit of reaching outside of ourselves with joy and enthusiasm.

Luci Swindoll

—Your Thoughts for Today—

_____

_____

_____

_____

_____

_____

_____

HIS TRANSFORMING POWER

Your old life is dead. Your new life, which is your real life—
even though invisible to spectators—is with Christ in God.
He is your life.

Colossians 3:3 MSG

God's hand has the power to transform your day, your life, and your health. Your task is to accept Christ's grace with a humble, thankful heart as you receive the "new life" that can be yours through Him.

Do you desire to improve some aspect of your life? If so, don't expect changing circumstances to miraculously transform you into the person you want to become. Transformation starts with God, and it starts in the quiet corners of a willing human heart—like yours.

God uses every cloud which comes in our physical life, in our moral or spiritual life, or in our circumstances, to bring us nearer to him until we come to the place where our Lord Jesus Christ lived, and we do not allow our hearts to be troubled.

Oswald Chambers

—Your Thoughts for Today—

_____

_____

_____

_____

_____

COMMISSIONED TO WITNESS

Go, therefore, and make disciples of all nations, baptizing them in the name of the Father and of the Son and of the Holy Spirit, teaching them to observe everything I have commanded you. And remember, I am with you always, to the end of the age.

Matthew 28:19-20 Holman CSB

After His resurrection, Jesus addressed His disciples. As recorded in the 28th chapter of Matthew, Christ instructed His followers to share His message with the world. This "Great Commission" applies to Christians of every generation, including our own.

As believers, we are called to share the Good News of Jesus with our families, with our neighbors, and with the world. Christ commanded His disciples to become fishers of men. We must do likewise, and we must do so today. Tomorrow may indeed be too late.

Witnessing is not something that we do for the Lord; it is something that He does through us if we are filled with the Holy Spirit.

Warren Wiersbe

—Your Thoughts for Today—

ABOUT DEPRESSION

Throughout our lives, all of us must endure personal challenges that leave us struggling to find hope. The sadness that accompanies such losses is an inescapable fact of life—but in time, we move beyond our grief as the sadness runs its course and life returns to normal. Depression, however, is more than sadness . . . much more.

Depression is a physical and emotional condition that is, in almost all cases, treatable with medication and counseling. And it is not a disease to be taken lightly. Left untreated, depression presents real dangers to patients' physical health and to their emotional well-being.

If you're feeling blue, perhaps it's a logical response to the disappointments of everyday life. But if your feelings of sadness have lasted longer than you think they should—or if someone close to you fears that your sadness may have evolved into clinical depression—it's time to seek professional help.

Here are a few simple guidelines to consider as you make decisions about possible medical treatment:

1. If your feelings of sadness have resulted in persistent and prolonged changes in sleep patterns, or if you've experience a significant change in weight (either gain or loss), consult your physician.

2. If you have persistent urges toward self-destructive behavior, or if you feel as though you have lost the will to live, consult a professional counselor or physician immediately.

3. If someone you trust urges you to seek counseling, schedule a session with a professionally trained counselor to evaluate your condition.

4. If you are plagued by consistent, prolonged, severe feelings of hopelessness, consult a physician, a professional counselor, or your pastor.

God's Word has much to say about every aspect of your life, including your emotional health. And, when you face concerns of any sort—including symptoms of depression—remember that God is with you. Your Creator Father intends that His joy should become your joy. Yet sometimes, amid the inevitable hustle and bustle of life, you may forfeit—albeit temporarily—God's joy as you wrestle with the challenges of daily living.

So, if you're feeling genuinely depressed, trust your medical doctor to do his or her part. Then, place your ultimate trust in your benevolent Heavenly Father. His healing touch, like His love, endures forever.

These things I have spoken to you,
that in Me you may have peace.
In the world you will have tribulation;
but be of good cheer,
I have overcome the world.

—

John 16:33 NKJV

WILEY & GRAMPA'S
CREATURE FEATURES
DRACULA vs. GRAMPA

AT THE MONSTER TRUCK SPECTACULAR

WRITTEN AND
ILLUSTRATED BY

KIRK
SCROGGS

LITTLE, BROWN AND COMPANY
New York · Boston · London

This book is for Harold & Betty & Diane & Corey
And is in memory of Guy Scroggs
and Charles Scroggs, master monster drawer and cool dad.

———

Special thanks—
Suppasak Viboonlarp, Mark Mayes, Kris Gee, Simeon Wilkens,
Jackie Greed, Rosa Jimenez, Amy Pennington, Inge Govaerts, Michael Moss

Andrea, Sangeeta, Saho and the Little, Brown crew—woo hoo!

And special super-duper deep-fried thanks with ranch seasoning to
Ashley & Carolyn Grayson and Dan Hooker

Little, Brown and Company

Time Warner Book Group
1271 Avenue of the Americas, New York, NY 10020
Visit our Web site at www.lb-kids.com

First Edition: July 2006

Library of Congress Cataloging-in-Publication Data

Scroggs, Kirk.
    Dracula vs. Grampa at the Monster Truck Spectacular/written and illustrated by Kirk
Scroggs.—1st ed.
    p. cm.—(Wiley & Grampa's creature features; #1)
    Summary: When Grampa and Wiley sneak out of the house on a stormy Halloween night
to attend Colonel Dracula's Monster Truck Spectacular, they run into trouble from which
only Gramma and an F5 tornado can save them.
    ISBN 0-316-05902-1 (hc) / 0-316-05941-2 (pb)
    [1. Grandparents—Fiction. 2. Vampires—Fiction. 3. Halloween—Fiction. 4. Humorous
stories.] I. Title.

PZ7.S436726Dra2006
[Fic]—dc22

                                                                        2005044436

10 9 8 7 6 5 4 3 2 1

CW

Printed in the United States of America

Book design by Saho Fujii

The illustrations for this book were done in Staedtler ink on Canson Marker paper,
then digitized with Adobe Photoshop for color and shade.
The text was set in Humana Sans Light and the display type was handlettered.